One Pot&Stews

One Pot&Stews

Amazingly tasty...surprisingly simple!

First published in 2010
LOVE FOOD is an imprint of Parragon Books Ltd

Parragon
Queen Street House
4 Queen Street
Bath BA1 1HE, UK

ISBN: 978-1-4075-5383-2

Printed in China

Cover design by Andrew Easton @ Ummagumma
Internal design by Ignition
Additional photography by Mike Cooper
Additional food styling by Lincoln Jefferson

Notes for the Reader

• This book uses imperial, metric, and US cup measurements. Follow the same units of measurement throughout; do not mix imperial and metric. All spoon measurements are level: teaspoons are assumed to be 5 ml, and tablespoons are assumed to be 15 ml. Unless otherwise stated, milk is assumed to be whole, eggs and individual vegetables are medium, and pepper is freshly ground black pepper.

• The times given are an approximate guide only. Preparation times differ according to the techniques used by different people and the cooking times may also vary from those given. Optional ingredients, variations, or serving suggestions have not been included in the calculations.

• Recipes using raw or very lightly cooked eggs should be avoided by infants, the elderly, pregnant women, convalescents, and anyone with a chronic illness. Pregnant and breast-feeding women are advised to avoid eating peanuts and peanut products. People with a nut allergy should be aware that some of the prepared ingredients used in the recipes in this book may contain nuts. Always check the packaging before use.

• Vegetarians should be aware that some of the prepared ingredients used in this book may contain animal products. Always check the packaging before use.

These days most of us lead action-packed lives, either at work or as a busy parent, or both. Time-consuming meal preparation, let alone cleaning up afterward, just doesn't fit in very easily. Yet most of us care about health and want to eat nutritious home-cooked food.

As the recipes in the book demonstrate, this no-frills way of cooking is the ultimate in terms of convenience because everything is ready at the same time. It's the ideal food for solitary suppers or for feeding a crowd. Just put the pot on the table and dig in.

GETTING STARTED

Before you start to cook:
• Read the recipe all the way through, then plan the sequence according to what needs soaking, chopping, precooking etc.
• Have the right tools and cookware on hand
• Make sure knives are sharp
• Wash fresh vegetables, fruits, and herbs
• Assemble all the ingredients, then measure or weigh them as necessary
• Complete any preparation, such as chopping or grating
• Have the prepared ingredients lined up in bowls, ready to add to the pot at the correct time
• Clean up as you work.

USEFUL UTENSILS

As well as basics, such as knives and cutting boards, there are a number of additional utensils that make one-pot cooking easier and safer.
• Though you can leave the pot to simmer while you are doing something else, it's still important to keep track of temperature and time. Thermometers are essential for food safety, and a timer with a loud ring is invaluable for reminding you when the dish needs your attention. You'll also need spoons and spatulas for stirring, and tools for turning and lifting ingredients that are precooked in stages before they go into the pot. A sturdy long-handled fork or multipronged meat lifter are handy for large pieces of meat, while stainless steel spring-action tongs let you clasp smaller pieces of food securely.

A perforated shallow skimmer is useful for removing froth and foam from the surface of stews.
• Although one-pot recipes are infinitely flexible, it's worth investing in proper kitchen measuring spoons and cups, especially if you are new to cooking. Once you gain experience and confidence, it's fine to add a pinch of this and a handful of that.
• The joy of one-pot meals is that they can be brought straight from oven to table.

COOKWARE

For most of the recipes in this book, a few heavy-bottom saucepans and casseroles in varying sizes with tight-fitting lids make up the basic equipment. You'll also need a deep skillet, a wok, good-quality roasting pans that won't warp or twist, and some shallow ovenproof dishes for gratins and crumbles.

FRESH PRODUCE

Wholesome fresh vegetables, meat, poultry, and fish add valuable nutrients to one-pot meals, as well as color, texture, and appetizing flavors.

Vegetables

These are one of the most important sources of vitamins, minerals, and fiber. Vegetables are packed with carotenoids (the plant form of vitamin A), vitamin C, and vitamin E, which collectively protect against heart disease and some cancers.

Meat and Poultry

Meat and poultry provide high-quality protein, important minerals, such as iron and zinc, and B vitamins, needed to release energy from food. Meat tends to be high in fat, so if you're trying to cut down, trim off any excess or choose lean cuts.

Fish and Seafood

Dense-fleshed fish and seafood make marvelous one-pot meals. They provide protein and essential minerals, while oily fish, such as tuna, are a unique source of omega-3 fatty acids that protect against heart disease and feed the brain.

Fresh Herbs

A generous sprinkling of fresh herbs added at the end of cooking will provide delightful fragrance and color to one-pot meals.

Beef Stock
Makes 7½ cups

2 lb 4 oz/1 kg beef marrow bones, sawn into
   3-inch/7.5-cm pieces
1 lb 7 oz/650 g stewing beef in a single piece
12½ cups water
4 cloves
2 onions, halved
2 celery stalks, roughly chopped
8 peppercorns
1 bouquet garni

• Put the bones in a large, heavy-bottom saucepan
and put the stewing beef on top. Pour in the water
and bring to a boil over low heat. Skim off the foam
that rises to the surface.
• Press a clove into each onion half and add to the
pan with the celery, peppercorns, and bouquet
garni. Partially cover and simmer gently for 3 hours.
Remove the stewing beef from the pan, partially
re-cover, and simmer for an additional hour.
• Remove the pan from the heat and let cool.
Strain the stock into a bowl, cover with plastic wrap,
and chill in the refrigerator for at least 1 hour or
preferably overnight.
• Remove and discard the layer of fat that has set
on the surface. Use immediately or freeze for up to
6 months.

Chicken Stock
Makes 10½ cups

3 lb/1.3 kg chicken wings and necks
2 onions, cut into wedges
17 cups water
2 carrots, roughly chopped
2 celery stalks, roughly chopped
10 fresh parsley sprigs
4 fresh thyme sprigs
2 bay leaves
10 black peppercorns

• Place the chicken and onions in a large, heavy-
bottom saucepan and cook over low heat, stirring
frequently, until browned all over.
• Pour in the water and stir well, scraping up any
sediment from the bottom of the pan. Bring to a boil
and skim off the foam that rises to the surface.
• Add the carrots, celery, parsley, thyme, bay leaves,
and peppercorns, partially cover the pan, and
simmer gently, stirring occasionally, for 3 hours.
• Remove the pan from the heat and let cool.
Strain the stock into a bowl, cover with plastic wrap,
and chill in the refrigerator for at least 1 hour or
preferably overnight.

• Remove and discard the layer of fat that has set
on the surface. Use immediately or freeze for up to
6 months.

Fish Stock
Makes 5½ cups

1 lb 7 oz/650 g white fish heads, bones,
   and trimmings
1 onion, sliced
2 celery stalks, chopped
1 carrot, sliced
1 bay leaf
4 fresh parsley sprigs
4 black peppercorns
½ lemon, sliced
½ cup white wine
5½ cups water

• Cut out and discard the gills from the fish heads,
then rinse the heads, bones, and trimmings. Place
them in a large, heavy-bottom saucepan.
• Add all the remaining ingredients. Bring to a boil
and skim off the foam that rises to the surface. Lower
the heat, partially cover, and simmer gently for
25 minutes.
• Remove the pan from the heat and let cool. Strain
the stock into a bowl, without pressing down on the
contents of the colander.
• Use immediately or freeze for up to 3 months.

Vegetable Stock
Makes 8½ cups

2 tbsp sunflower or corn oil
1 onion, finely chopped
1⅓ cups finely chopped leeks
2 carrots, finely chopped
4 celery stalks, finely chopped
¾ cup finely chopped fennel
1 tomato finely chopped
10 cups water
1 bouquet garni

• Heat the oil in a large, heavy-bottom saucepan.
Add the onions and leeks and cook over low heat,
stirring occasionally, for 5 minutes, until softened.
• Add the carrots, celery, fennel, and tomatoes,
cover, and cook, stirring occasionally, for 10 minutes.
Pour in the water, add the bouquet garni, and
bring to a boil. Lower the heat and simmer for
20 minutes.
• Remove the pan from the heat and let cool. Strain
the stock into a bowl. Use immediately or freeze for
up to 3 months.

Soups

SERVES 6

2 carrots, sliced
1 onion, diced
1 garlic clove, crushed
8 small new potatoes, diced
2 celery stalks, sliced
1²/₃ cups quartered button mushrooms

14 oz/400 g canned chopped tomatoes in tomato juice
2½ cups vegetable stock
1 bay leaf
1 tsp dried mixed herbs or 1 tbsp chopped fresh mixed herbs

½ cup corn kernels, frozen or canned, drained
²/₃ cup shredded green cabbage
pepper
crusty whole wheat or white bread rolls, to serve

Chunky Vegetable Soup

Put the carrots, onion, garlic, potatoes, celery, mushrooms, tomatoes, and stock into a large pan. Stir in the bay leaf and herbs. Bring to a boil, then reduce the heat, cover, and let simmer for 25 minutes.

Add the corn and cabbage and return to a boil. Reduce the heat, cover, and simmer for 5 minutes, or until the vegetables are tender. Remove and discard the bay leaf. Season to taste with pepper.

Ladle into warmed bowls and serve at once with crusty bread rolls.

SERVES 4

2 tbsp olive oil
1 onion, chopped
1 garlic clove, chopped
1 tbsp chopped fresh
  ginger

1 small red chile, seeded
  and finely chopped
2 tbsp chopped fresh
  cilantro
1 bay leaf

2 lb 4 oz/1 kg pumpkin,
  peeled, seeded, and
  diced
2½ cups vegetable stock
salt and pepper
light cream, to garnish

Spiced Pumpkin Soup

Heat the oil in a pan over medium heat. Add the onion and garlic and cook, stirring, for about 4 minutes, until slightly softened. Add the ginger, chile, cilantro, bay leaf, and pumpkin, and cook for another 3 minutes.

Pour in the stock and bring to a boil. Using a slotted spoon, skim any foam from the surface. Reduce the heat and simmer gently, stirring occasionally, for about 25 minutes, or until the pumpkin is tender. Remove from the heat, take out the bay leaf, and let cool a little.

Transfer the soup into a food processor or blender and process until smooth (you may have to do this in batches). Return the mixture to the rinsed-out pan and season to taste with salt and pepper. Reheat gently, stirring. Remove from the heat, pour into warmed soup bowls, garnish each one with a swirl of cream, and serve.

SERVES 4

3 tbsp olive oil
2 onions, chopped
2 garlic cloves, chopped
2 large red bell peppers,
 seeded and chopped

1 lb 2 oz/500 g ripe
 tomatoes, chopped
½ cup red lentils
2½ cups vegetable stock,
 plus extra for thinning
 (optional)

1 tbsp red wine vinegar
salt and pepper
2 scallions, chopped, or
 1 tbsp snipped fresh
 chives, for garnish

Tomato, Lentil + Red Bell Pepper Soup

Heat the oil in a large skillet over medium–high heat, then add the onions and cook, stirring, for 5 minutes, or until softened but not browned. Add the garlic and bell peppers and cook, stirring, for 5 minutes, or until the bell peppers are softened.

Add the tomatoes, lentils, and stock and bring to a simmer. Reduce the heat to low, then cover and simmer gently for 25 minutes, or until the lentils are tender. Stir in the vinegar and season to taste with salt and pepper.

Let cool slightly, then transfer the soup to a blender or food processor and blend for 1 minute, or until smooth. Return to the skillet and reheat, stirring in a little hot water or stock if the soup seems a little too thick.

Serve in warmed bowls, garnished with the scallions.

SERVES 4

2 tbsp olive oil
1 onion, chopped
2 celery stalks, chopped
1 large carrot, coarsely
  chopped

1 large or 2 small sweet
  potatoes, peeled and
  chopped
14 oz/400 g canned lima
  beans or cannellini
  beans, drained
  and rinsed

4 cups vegetable stock
salt and pepper
2 tbsp freshly grated
  Parmesan cheese,
  to serve
1 large handful fresh
  cilantro leaves,
  to garnish

Chunky Sweet Potato & Lima Bean Soup

Heat the oil in a large saucepan over medium heat, then add the onion, celery, and carrot and cook, stirring frequently, for 8–10 minutes, or until softened. Add the sweet potatoes and beans and cook, stirring, for 1 minute.

Add the stock, then stir thoroughly and bring to a simmer. Season to taste with salt and pepper. Cover, then reduce the heat and cook for 25–30 minutes, or until all the vegetables are tender.

Let cool slightly, then transfer one-third of the soup to a blender or food processor and blend until smooth. Return to the saucepan and mix in well. Check the seasoning and reheat.

Ladle into warmed bowls and scatter with the Parmesan cheese and cilantro before serving.

SERVES 6

generous 1 cup dried red split lentils
1 red onion, diced
2 large carrots, sliced
1 celery stalk, sliced
1 parsnip, diced

1 garlic clove, crushed
5 cups vegetable stock
2 tsp paprika
pepper
6 tbsp lowfat plain mascarpone cheese (optional)

1 tbsp snipped fresh chives, to garnish
crusty whole wheat or white bread

Red Lentil Soup

Put the lentils, onion, vegetables, garlic, stock, and paprika into a large pan. Bring to a boil and boil rapidly for 10 minutes. Reduce the heat, cover, and let simmer for 20 minutes, or until the lentils and vegetables are tender.

Let the soup cool slightly, then puree in small batches in a food processor or blender. Process until the mixture is smooth.

Return the soup to the pan and heat through thoroughly. Season to taste with pepper.

To serve, ladle the soup into warmed bowls and swirl in a tablespoonful of mascarpone cheese, if desired. Sprinkle the chives over the soup to garnish and serve at once with crusty bread.

SERVES 4

2 tbsp peanut oil
1 lb/450 g stewing beef
2 celery stalks, chopped
1 medium onion, chopped
2 tsp finely chopped fresh ginger
¼ cup pearl barley
2 star anise

½ cinnamon stick
2 cloves
1 tsp chipotle powder, or to taste
4 cups/950 ml low-sodium beef stock
5 cups water
2 tbsp Thai fish sauce, or to taste

1 tbsp fresh lime juice, or to taste
¼ cup chopped fresh cilantro
¼ cup chopped fresh mint
2 scallions, finely chopped

Beef + Barley Soup

In a large saucepan, heat the oil over medium–high heat. Add the beef and cook for about 10 minutes, until browned on all sides. Using a slotted spoon, remove the beef from the pan and place in a bowl. Reduce the heat to medium, add the celery, onion, ginger, and barley, and sauté for about 10 minutes, until the onion is softened and golden. Add the star anise, cinnamon stick, cloves, and chipotle powder and cook for about 2 minutes, until aromatic.

Return the beef to the pan, add the beef stock, water, and fish sauce, and bring to a boil. Reduce the heat and simmer, uncovered, for about 1–1½ hours, or until the beef is tender. Using a slotted spoon, remove the beef from the pan. Cool slightly, then shred the meat. Return the beef to the pan and cook to heat through. Add the lime juice. Taste and add additional fish sauce or lime juice, if needed. Stir in the cilantro, mint, and scallions. Spoon into soup bowls and serve.

SERVES 4

2 tbsp vegetable oil
1 large onion, finely chopped
2 garlic cloves, finely chopped
1 green bell pepper, seeded and sliced

2 carrots, sliced
14 oz/400 g canned black-eyed peas
8 oz/225 g fresh ground beef
1 tsp each ground cumin, chili powder, and paprika

¼ head of cabbage, sliced
2 tomatoes, peeled and chopped
2½ cups beef stock
salt and pepper

Beef + Bean Soup

Heat the oil in a large pan over medium heat. Add the onion and garlic and cook, stirring frequently, for 3 minutes, or until softened. Add the bell pepper and carrots and cook for an additional 5 minutes.

Meanwhile, drain the peas, reserving the liquid from the can. Place two-thirds of the peas, reserving the remainder, in a food processor or blender with the pea liquid and process until smooth.

Add the ground beef to the pan and cook, stirring constantly to break up any lumps, until well browned. Add the spices and cook, stirring, for 2 minutes. Add the cabbage, tomatoes, stock, and processed peas and season to taste with salt and pepper. Bring to a boil, then reduce the heat, cover, and simmer for 15 minutes, or until the vegetables are tender.

Stir in the reserved peas, cover, and simmer for an additional 5 minutes. Ladle the soup into warmed soup bowls and serve.

SERVES 4

5½ oz/150 g lean beef
scant ¼ cup rice
3½ cups beef stock
1 leek, sliced

1 garlic clove, thinly
  sliced
2 tsp light soy sauce
1 tsp rice wine vinegar

1 medium open-cap
  mushroom, thinly sliced
salt

Beef + Rice Soup

Using a sharp knife, trim any visible fat from the beef and cut the meat into thin strips. Set aside until required.

Bring a large pan of lightly salted water to a boil and add the rice. Return to a boil, stir once, reduce the heat, and cook for 10–15 minutes, or until tender. Drain the cooked rice, rinse under cold running water, drain again, and set aside.

Place the beef stock in a large pan and bring to a boil. Add the beef strips, leek, garlic, soy sauce, and rice wine vinegar, reduce the heat, cover, and let simmer for 10 minutes, or until the beef is tender and cooked through.

Add the mushroom slices and cooked rice to the pan and cook for an additional 2–3 minutes, or until the mushrooms are completely cooked through.

Ladle the soup into warmed bowls and serve immediately.

SERVES 4–6

1–2 tbsp olive oil
1 lb/450 g lean boneless beef
1 onion, finely chopped
2–3 garlic cloves, crushed
5 cups water
14 oz/400 g canned chopped tomatoes
1 bay leaf

½ tsp each dried thyme and oregano
⅛ tsp ground cinnamon
¼ tsp each ground cumin and turmeric
1 tsp harissa, or more to taste
14 oz/400 g canned chickpeas

1 carrot, diced
1 potato, diced
1 zucchini, quartered lengthwise and sliced
⅔ cup fresh or defrosted frozen peas
salt and pepper
sprigs of fresh mint or cilantro, to garnish

Spicy Beef + Chickpea Soup

Heat 1 tablespoon of the oil in a large saucepan or cast-iron casserole over medium–high heat. Cut the beef into cubes and add to the pan, in batches if necessary to avoid overcrowding, and cook until evenly browned on all sides, adding a little more oil, if needed. Remove the meat with a slotted spoon when browned.

Reduce the heat and add the onion and garlic to the pan. Cook, stirring frequently, for 1–2 minutes.

Add the water and return all the meat to the pan. Bring just to a boil and skim off any foam that rises to the surface. Reduce the heat and stir in the tomatoes, bay leaf, thyme, oregano, cinnamon, cumin, turmeric, and harissa. Simmer for about 1 hour, or until the meat is very tender. Discard the bay leaf.

Rinse and drain the chickpeas, then stir into the pan with the carrot and potato and simmer for 15 minutes. Add the zucchini and peas and continue simmering for 15–20 minutes, or until all the vegetables are tender.

Season to taste with salt and pepper, adding more harissa, if desired. Ladle the soup into warmed bowls and garnish with mint or cilantro.

SERVES 4

1 tbsp chili oil
1 garlic clove, chopped
3 scallions, sliced
1 red bell pepper, seeded and finely sliced
2 tbsp cornstarch
4 cups vegetable stock
1 tbsp soy sauce

2 tbsp rice wine or dry sherry
5½ oz/150 g pork tenderloin, sliced
1 tbsp finely chopped lemongrass
1 small red chile, seeded and finely chopped

1 tbsp grated fresh ginger
4 oz/115 g fine egg noodles
7 oz/200 g canned water chestnuts, drained and sliced
salt and pepper

Pork & Vegetable Broth

Heat the oil in a large pan. Add the garlic and scallions and cook over medium heat, stirring, for 3 minutes, until slightly softened. Add the bell pepper and cook for an additional 5 minutes, stirring.

In a bowl, mix the cornstarch with enough of the stock to make a smooth paste and stir it into the pan. Cook, stirring, for 2 minutes. Stir in the remaining stock with the soy sauce and rice wine, then add the pork, lemongrass, chile, and ginger. Season to taste with salt and pepper. Bring to a boil, then lower the heat and simmer for 25 minutes.

Bring a separate pan of water to a boil, add the noodles, and cook for 3 minutes. Remove from the heat, drain, then add the noodles to the soup along with the water chestnuts. Cook for another 2 minutes, then remove from the heat and ladle into serving bowls.

SERVES 6–8

2²/₃ cups split green peas
1 tbsp olive oil
1 large onion, finely
chopped
1 large carrot, finely
chopped

1 celery stalk, finely
chopped
4 cups chicken or
vegetable stock
4 cups water
8 oz/225 g lean smoked
ham, finely diced

¼ tsp dried thyme
¼ tsp dried marjoram
1 bay leaf
salt and pepper

Split Pea & Ham Soup

Rinse the peas under cold running water. Put in a saucepan and cover generously with water. Bring to a boil and boil for 3 minutes, skimming off the foam from the surface. Drain the peas.

Heat the oil in a large saucepan over medium heat. Add the onion and cook for 3–4 minutes, stirring occasionally, until just softened.

Add the carrot and celery and continue cooking for 2 minutes. Add the peas, pour in the stock and water, and stir to combine.

Bring just to a boil and stir the ham into the soup. Add the thyme, marjoram, and bay leaf. Reduce the heat, cover, and cook gently for 1–1½ hours, until the ingredients are very soft. Remove the bay leaf.

Taste and adjust the seasoning, if necessary. Ladle into warmed soup bowls and serve.

SERVES 4

1 lb/450 g thick, rindless smoked bacon strips, diced
1 onion, chopped
2 carrots, sliced

2 celery stalks, chopped
1 turnip, chopped
1 large potato, chopped
generous 2¼ cups French green lentils

1 bouquet garni
4 cups chicken stock
salt and pepper

Bacon + Lentil Soup

Heat a large, heavy-bottom saucepan or flameproof casserole. Add the bacon and cook over medium heat, stirring, for 4–5 minutes, or until the fat runs. Add the chopped onion, carrots, celery, turnip, and potato and cook, stirring frequently, for 5 minutes.

Add the lentils and bouquet garni and pour in the stock. Bring to a boil, reduce the heat, and simmer for 1 hour, or until the lentils are tender.

Remove and discard the bouquet garni, taste the soup, and adjust the seasoning, if necessary. Ladle into warmed soup bowls and serve.

SERVES 4

2 tbsp olive oil
2 garlic cloves, chopped
2 red onions, chopped
1 red bell pepper, seeded
and chopped
2 tbsp cornstarch

4 cups vegetable stock
4 potatoes, peeled,
halved, and sliced
5½ oz/150 g chorizo,
sliced
2 zucchini, trimmed and
sliced

7 oz/200 g canned red
kidney beans, rinsed
and drained
½ cup heavy cream
salt and pepper

Chorizo & Red Kidney Bean Soup

Heat the oil in a large pan. Add the garlic and onions and cook over medium heat, stirring, for 3 minutes, until slightly softened. Add the bell pepper and cook for another 3 minutes, stirring. In a bowl, mix the cornstarch with enough stock to make a smooth paste and stir it into the pan. Cook, stirring, for 2 minutes. Stir in the remaining stock, then add the potatoes and season to taste with salt and pepper. Bring to a boil, then lower the heat and simmer for 25 minutes, until the vegetables are tender.

Add the chorizo, zucchini, and kidney beans to the pan. Cook for 10 minutes, then stir in the cream and cook for another 5 minutes. Remove from the heat and ladle into serving bowls.

SERVES 4

3 tbsp butter
4 shallots, chopped
1 leek, sliced
1 lb/450 g skinless,
  boneless chicken
  breasts, chopped

2½ cups chicken stock
1 tbsp chopped fresh
  parsley
1 tbsp chopped fresh
  thyme, plus extra sprigs
  to garnish

¾ cup heavy cream
salt and pepper

Cream of Chicken Soup

Melt the butter in a large pan over medium heat. Add the shallots and cook, stirring, for 3 minutes, until slightly softened. Add the leek and cook for another 5 minutes, stirring. Add the chicken, stock, and herbs, and season to taste with salt and pepper. Bring to a boil, then lower the heat and simmer for 25 minutes, until the chicken is tender and cooked through. Remove from the heat and cool for 10 minutes.

Transfer the soup into a food processor or blender and process until smooth (you may need to do this in batches). Return the soup to the rinsed-out pan and warm over low heat for 5 minutes.

Stir in the cream and cook for another 2 minutes, then remove from the heat and ladle into serving bowls. Garnish with sprigs of thyme and serve immediately.

SERVES 4–6

1–2 tbsp olive oil
2 onions, finely chopped
1–2 red chiles, seeded
   and finely chopped
1 tsp ground cumin
1 tsp paprika
1 tsp granulated sugar
2 tsp dried mint

1 tbsp tomato paste
5 cups chicken stock
½ cup couscous
1 chicken, weighing
   3 lb/1.3 kg, cooked
   and roughly torn into
   strips

salt and pepper
2 tbsp finely chopped
   cilantro, to garnish
1 lemon, quartered,
   to serve

Chicken Soup with Chile, Mint & Couscousa

Heat the oil in a heavy-bottom saucepan, add the onions and chiles, and cook over medium heat for 2–3 minutes, stirring frequently, until they begin to color.

Add the cumin, paprika, sugar, mint, and tomato paste, and pour in the chicken stock. Bring to a boil and gradually stir in the couscous. Reduce the heat and simmer for 15 minutes. Stir in the strips of chicken, taste and adjust the seasoning, if necessary, and simmer for an additional 5 minutes.

Garnish the soup with the cilantro and serve with the lemon quarters for squeezing over.

SERVES 4

4 tbsp butter
1 large onion, chopped
1 leek, trimmed and
    sliced

2⅓ cups sliced, cooked
    turkey
2½ cups chicken stock
5½ oz/150 g bleu cheese
⅔ cup heavy cream

1 tbsp chopped fresh
    tarragon
pepper
fresh tarragon leaves and
    croutons, to garnish

Turkey, Leek & Bleu Cheese Soup

Melt the butter in a pan over medium heat. Add the onion and cook, stirring, for 4 minutes, until slightly softened. Add the leek and cook for another 3 minutes.

Add the turkey to the pan and pour in the stock. Bring to a boil, then reduce the heat and simmer gently, stirring occasionally, for about 15 minutes. Remove from the heat and let cool a little.

Transfer half of the soup into a food processor and blend until smooth. Return the mixture to the pan with the rest of the soup, stir in the bleu cheese, cream, and tarragon, and season to taste with pepper. Reheat gently, stirring. Remove from the heat, ladle into warmed soup bowls, garnish with tarragon and croutons, and serve.

SERVES 2

2 duck breasts, skin on
2 tbsp red curry paste
2 tbsp vegetable oil or
   peanut oil
bunch of scallions,
   chopped

2 garlic cloves, crushed
2-inch/5-cm piece fresh
   ginger, grated
2 carrots, thinly sliced
1 red bell pepper, seeded
   and cut into strips

4 cups chicken stock
2 tbsp sweet chili sauce
3–4 tbsp Thai soy sauce
14 oz/400 g canned
   straw mushrooms,
   drained

Duck with Scallion Soup

Slash the skin of the duck 3–4 times with a sharp knife and rub in the curry paste. Cook the duck breasts, skin-side down, in a wok or skillet over high heat for 2–3 minutes. Turn over, reduce the heat, and cook for an additional 3–4 minutes, until cooked through. Lift out and slice thickly. Set aside and keep warm.

Meanwhile, heat the oil in a wok or large skillet and stir-fry half the scallions with the garlic, ginger, carrots, and bell pepper for 2–3 minutes. Pour in the stock and add the chili sauce, soy sauce, and mushrooms. Bring to a boil, reduce the heat, and simmer for 4–5 minutes.

Ladle the soup into warmed bowls, top with the duck slices, and garnish with the remaining scallions. Serve immediately.

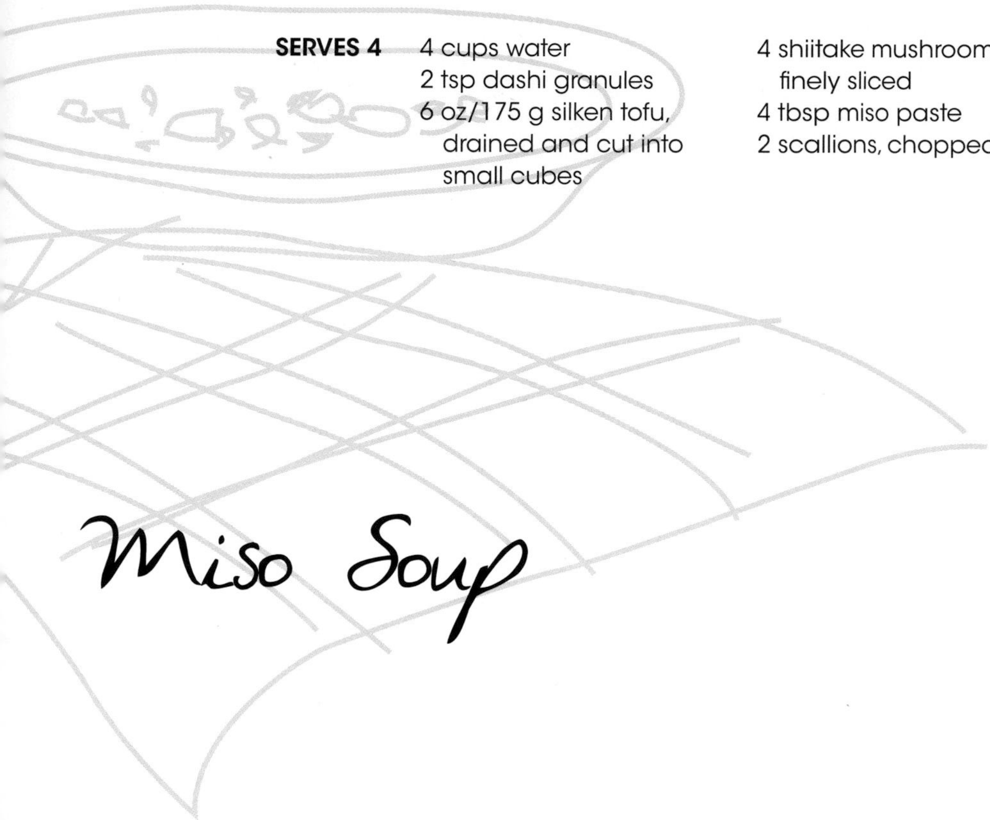

SERVES 4

4 cups water
2 tsp dashi granules
6 oz/175 g silken tofu,
    drained and cut into
    small cubes

4 shiitake mushrooms,
    finely sliced
4 tbsp miso paste
2 scallions, chopped

Miso Soup

Put the water in a large pan with the dashi granules and bring to a boil. Add the tofu and mushrooms, reduce the heat, and simmer for 3 minutes.

Stir in the miso paste and simmer gently, stirring, until it has dissolved.

Add the scallions and serve immediately. If you leave the soup, the miso will settle, so stir the soup thoroughly before serving to recombine.

SERVES 4

2 tbsp olive oil
3 strips smoked, fatty
  bacon, chopped
2 tbsp butter
4 starchy potatoes,
  chopped

3 onions, finely chopped
2½ cups chicken stock
2½ cups milk
3½ oz/100 g dried
  conchigliette
  (small pasta shells)

⅔ cup heavy cream
2 tbsp chopped fresh
  parsley
2 tbsp pesto
salt and pepper
freshly grated Parmesan
  cheese, to serve

Potato & Pesto Soup

Heat the oil in a large saucepan and cook the bacon over medium heat for
4 minutes. Add the butter, potatoes, and onions, and cook for 12 minutes, stirring
constantly.

Add the stock and milk to the pan, bring to a boil, and simmer for 5 minutes. Add
the conchigliette and simmer for an additional 3–5 minutes.

Blend in the cream and simmer for 5 minutes. Add the chopped parsley and pesto,
and season to taste with salt and pepper. Transfer the soup to individual serving
bowls and serve with Parmesan cheese.

SERVES 6

2 tbsp butter
1 onion, chopped
1 garlic clove, finely
  chopped
2 oz/55 g rindless bacon,
  diced
2 celery stalks, chopped

14 oz/400 g canned
  chopped tomatoes
⅔ cup dry white wine
1¼ cups fish stock
4 fresh basil leaves, torn
2 tbsp chopped fresh
  flat-leaf parsley

1 lb/450 g whitefish fillets,
  such as halibut or
  monkfish, skinned and
  chopped
4 oz/115 g cooked
  peeled shrimp
salt and pepper

Genoese Fish Soup

Melt the butter in a large, heavy-bottom saucepan. Add the onion and garlic and cook over low heat, stirring occasionally, for 5 minutes, or until softened.

Add the bacon and celery and cook, stirring frequently, for an additional 2 minutes.

Add the tomatoes, wine, stock, basil, and 1 tablespoon of the parsley. Season to taste with salt and pepper. Bring to a boil, then reduce the heat and simmer for 10 minutes.

Add the whitefish and cook for 5 minutes, or until it is opaque. Add the shrimp and heat through gently for 3 minutes. Ladle into warmed serving bowls, garnish with the remaining chopped parsley, and serve immediately.

SERVES 4

4 tbsp olive oil
3 leeks, sliced
2 celery stalks, chopped
1 large onion, chopped
2 large garlic cloves, well crushed
9 oz/250 g cremini mushrooms, sliced
4 cups fish stock
9 oz/250 g canned tomatoes

scant ½ cup Italian dry white wine
1 tsp hot paprika
1 lb/450 g mixed fish fillets, such as halibut, bass, monkfish, red snapper, and sea bream, cut into bite-size pieces

1 lb/450 g mixed raw seafood, such as shrimp, mussels in their shells, squid, cut into rings and tentacles chopped, and crabmeat
salt and pepper
plenty of chopped fresh flat-leaf parsley, to garnish

Italian Fish Soup with White Wine

Heat the oil in a large saucepan or flameproof casserole over medium heat. Add the leeks, celery, onion, and garlic and cook, stirring frequently, for 8–10 minutes, or until softened. Add the mushrooms, stock, tomatoes and their juice, and wine and stir well.

Bring to a simmer, add the paprika, and season to taste with salt and pepper. Then add all the fish and seafood and simmer gently for 15 minutes. Check the seasoning.

Serve in warmed bowls, garnished with the parsley.

SERVES 4

1 tbsp olive oil
1 large onion, finely
  chopped
3 large leeks, including
  green parts, thinly
  sliced

1 potato, finely diced
2 cups fish stock
3 cups water
1 bay leaf
10½ oz/300 g skinless
  salmon fillet, cut into
  ½-inch/1-cm cubes

⅓ cup heavy cream
fresh lemon juice
  (optional)
salt and pepper
sprigs of fresh chervil or
  parsley, to garnish

Salmon & Leek Soup

Heat the oil in a large, heavy-bottom saucepan over medium heat. Add the onion and leeks and cook for about 3 minutes, until they begin to soften.

Add the potato, stock, water, and bay leaf with a large pinch of salt. Bring to a boil, reduce the heat, cover, and cook gently for about 25 minutes, or until the vegetables are tender. Remove the bay leaf.

Let the soup cool slightly, then transfer about half of it to a food processor or blender and process until smooth. Return the processed soup to the saucepan and stir to blend. Reheat gently over medium–low heat.

Season the salmon to taste with salt and pepper and add to the soup. Continue cooking for about 5 minutes, stirring occasionally, until the fish is tender and starts to break up. Stir in the cream, taste, and adjust the seasoning, adding a little lemon juice if desired. Ladle into warmed bowls, garnish with chervil or parsley, and serve.

SERVES 4

4 tsp butter
1 large onion, finely
  chopped
1 small carrot, finely
  diced
3 tbsp all-purpose flour

1¼ cups fish stock
¾ cup water
4 potatoes, diced
1 cup canned or
  defrosted frozen corn
  kernels

2 cups whole milk
10 oz/280 g canned
  clams, drained and
  rinsed
salt and pepper
chopped fresh parsley,
  to garnish

Clam & Corn Chowder

Melt the butter in a large saucepan over medium–low heat. Add the onion and carrot and cook for 3–4 minutes, stirring frequently, until the onion is softened. Stir in the flour and continue cooking for 2 minutes.

Slowly add about half the stock and stir well, scraping the bottom of the pan to mix in the flour. Pour in the remaining stock and the water and bring just to a boil, stirring.

Add the potatoes, corn, and milk and stir to combine. Reduce the heat and simmer gently, partially covered, for about 20 minutes, stirring occasionally, until all the vegetables are tender.

Chop the clams, if large. Stir in the clams and continue cooking for about 5 minutes, until heated through. Taste and adjust the seasoning, if needed.

Ladle the soup into bowls and sprinkle with parsley.

SERVES 4

20–24 large shrimp
2 cups fish stock
pinch of salt
1 tsp peanut oil
2 cups coconut milk
2 tsp nam pla
    (Thai fish sauce)
½ tbsp lime juice
4 oz/115 g dried medium
    rice noodles

⅓ cup bean sprouts
sprigs of fresh cilantro,
    to garnish

laksa paste
6 fresh cilantro stalks with
    leaves
3 large garlic cloves,
    crushed
1 fresh red chile, seeded
    and chopped

1 lemongrass stalk, center
    part only, chopped
1-inch/2.5-cm piece fresh
    ginger, peeled and
    chopped
1½ tbsp shrimp paste
½ tsp ground turmeric
2 tbsp peanut oil

Shrimp Laksa

Shell and devein the shrimp. Put the fish stock, salt, and the shrimp heads, shells, and tails in a large saucepan over high heat and bring to a boil. Lower the heat and simmer for 10 minutes, then remove from the heat. Transfer to a bowl and keep warm.

Meanwhile, make the laksa paste. Put all the ingredients except the oil in a food processor and blend. With the motor running, slowly add up to 2 tablespoons of oil just until a paste forms. (If your food processor is too large to work efficiently with this small quantity, use a mortar and pestle, or make double the quantity and keep leftovers tightly covered in the refrigerator to use another time.)

Heat the oil in the cleaned, large saucepan over high heat. Add the paste and stir-fry until it is fragrant. Strain the stock through a strainer lined with cheesecloth. Stir the stock into the laksa paste, along with the coconut milk, nam pla, and lime juice. Bring to a boil, then lower the heat, cover, and simmer for 30 minutes.

Meanwhile, soak the noodles in a large bowl with enough lukewarm water to cover for 20 minutes, until soft. Alternatively, cook according to the package instructions. Drain and set aside.

Add the shrimp and bean sprouts to the soup and continue simmering just until the shrimp turn opaque and curl. Divide the noodles among 4 bowls and ladle the soup over, making sure everyone gets an equal share of the shrimp. Garnish with the cilantro and serve.

SERVES 6

2 lb 4 oz/1 kg mussels
4 tbsp all-purpose flour
6¼ cups fish stock
1 tbsp butter

1 large onion, finely
   chopped
12 oz/350 g skinless
   whitefish fillets, such as
   cod, sole, or haddock

7 oz/200 g cooked or raw
   peeled shrimp
1¼ cups heavy cream
salt and pepper
snipped fresh dill,
   to garnish

Seafood Chowder

Discard any mussels with broken shells or any that refuse to close when tapped. Rinse and pull off any beards. Put the mussels in a large, heavy-bottom saucepan. Cover tightly and cook over high heat for about 4 minutes, or until the mussels open, shaking the pan occasionally. Discard any that remain closed. When they are cool enough to handle, remove the mussels from the shells and set aside.

Put the flour in a mixing bowl and very slowly whisk in enough of the stock to make a thick paste. Whisk in a little more stock to make a smooth liquid.

Melt the butter in a heavy-bottom saucepan over medium–low heat. Add the onion, cover, and cook for 3 minutes, stirring frequently, until it softens.

Add the remaining fish stock and bring to a boil. Slowly whisk in the flour mixture until well combined and bring back to a boil, whisking constantly. Add the mussel cooking liquid. Season with salt, if needed, and pepper. Reduce the heat and simmer, partially covered, for 15 minutes.

Add the whitefish and the mussels and continue simmering, stirring occasionally, for about 5 minutes, or until the fish is cooked and begins to flake.

Stir in the shrimp and cream. Taste and adjust the seasoning, if necessary. Simmer for 2–3 minutes longer to heat through. Ladle into warmed bowls, sprinkle with dill, and serve.

SERVES 2

10½ oz/300 g peeled shrimp
2 tsp vegetable oil
2 fresh red chiles, sliced
1 garlic clove, sliced
about 3 cups fish stock

4 thin slices fresh ginger
2 lemongrass stalks, bruised
5 Thai lime leaves, shredded
2 tsp jaggery or dark brown sugar

1 tbsp chili oil
handful of fresh cilantro leaves
dash of lime juice

Hot & Sour Shrimp Soup

Dry-fry the shrimp in a skillet or wok until they turn pink. Remove and set aside.

Heat the vegetable oil in the same skillet, add the chiles and garlic, and cook for 30 seconds.

Add the stock, ginger, lemongrass, Thai lime leaves, and sugar and simmer for 4 minutes. Add the reserved shrimp with the chili oil and cilantro and cook for 1–2 minutes.

Stir in the lime juice and serve immediately.

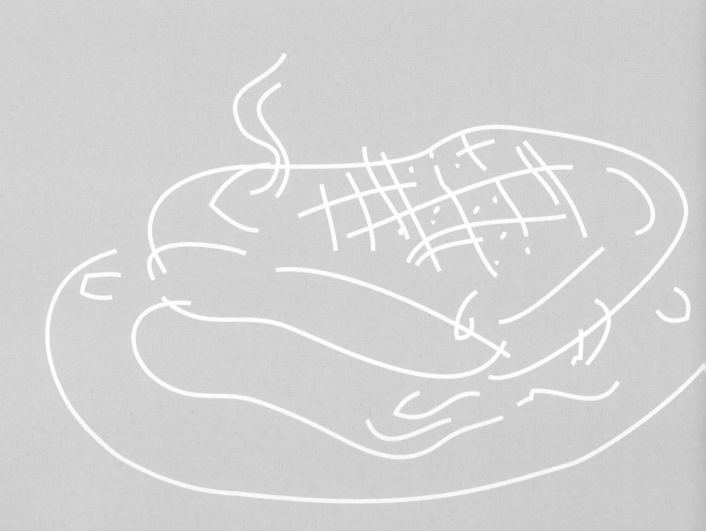

Meat & Poultry

SERVES 4–6

3 lb/1.3 kg braising beef, cubed
2 tbsp vegetable oil
4 onions, finely chopped
4 tbsp sweet paprika
2 tbsp tomato paste

1 tsp caraway or dill seeds
2 tsp wine vinegar
4 green bell peppers, seeded and diced
1 large garlic clove, finely chopped

5 medium potatoes, peeled and cubed
1½–1¾ cups hot meat stock
salt and pepper
3 tbsp chopped fresh dill
sour cream, to serve

Hungarian Beef Goulash

Put the meat in a shallow dish and sprinkle with 1 teaspoon of salt. Toss to mix, then cover and let stand for 15 minutes. Preheat the oven to 325°F/160°C.

Heat a Dutch oven over medium heat. Add the oil and gently cook the onions until softened but not colored. Season with another teaspoon of salt, then stir in the paprika and tomato paste and cook for a minute or two. Stir in the caraway seeds, vinegar, and ½ teaspoon of pepper. Add the bell peppers and garlic and cook for a few more minutes.

Add the meat to the pot, stirring well to coat. Cover tightly and cook in the oven for 1 hour, stirring every 30 minutes to submerge the meat in the juices (which should come slightly below the top of the meat). Add the potatoes and cook for another hour, stirring halfway through, until the meat is tender.

Pour in enough hot stock to come just above the meat. Cover and cook for another 20–30 minutes. Taste and adjust the seasoning, if necessary. Serve sprinkled with the chopped dill and a dollop of sour cream.

SERVES 6

2 tbsp corn oil
2 large onions, thinly
   sliced
8 carrots, sliced
4 tbsp all-purpose flour
2 lb 12 oz/1.25 kg
   braising beef, cut into
   cubes

generous 1¾ cups stout
   or dark beer
2 tsp brown sugar
2 bay leaves
1 tbsp chopped fresh
   thyme
salt and pepper

herb dumplings
generous ¾ cup
   self-rising flour
pinch of salt
½ cup lard, chilled and
   cut into small pieces
2 tbsp chopped fresh
   parsley, plus extra
   to garnish
about 4 tbsp water

Beef in Beer with Herb Dumplings

Preheat the oven to 325°F/160°C. Heat the oil in a flameproof casserole. Add the onions and carrots and cook over low heat, stirring occasionally, for 5 minutes, or until the onions are softened. Meanwhile, place the flour in a plastic bag and season with salt and pepper. Add the braising beef to the bag, tie the top, and shake well to coat. Do this in batches, if necessary.

Remove the vegetables from the casserole with a slotted spoon and reserve. Add the braising beef to the casserole, in batches, and cook, stirring frequently, until browned all over. Return all the meat and the onions and carrots to the casserole and sprinkle in any remaining seasoned flour. Pour in the stout and add the sugar, bay leaves, and thyme. Bring to a boil, cover, and transfer to the preheated oven to bake for 1¾ hours.

To make the herb dumplings, sift the flour and salt into a bowl. Stir in the lard and parsley and add enough of the water to make a soft dough. Shape into small balls between the palms of your hands. Add to the casserole and return to the oven for 30 minutes. Remove and discard the bay leaves and serve, sprinkled with parsley.

SERVES 4

1 lb/450 g braising beef
1½ tbsp all-purpose flour
1 tsp hot paprika
1–1½ tsp chili powder
1 tsp ground ginger
2 tbsp olive oil
1 large onion, cut into chunks

3 garlic cloves, sliced
2 celery stalks, sliced
4 carrots, chopped
1¼ cups beer
1¼ cups beef stock
3 potatoes, chopped
1 red bell pepper, seeded and chopped

2 corn cobs, halved
1 tomato, cut into quarters
1 cup shelled fresh or frozen peas
salt and pepper
1 tbsp chopped fresh cilantro

Beef & Vegetable Stew

Trim any fat or gristle from the beef and cut the meat into 1-inch/2.5-cm chunks. Mix the flour and spices together. Toss the beef in the spiced flour until well coated.

Heat the oil in a large, heavy-bottom pan and cook the onion, garlic, and celery, stirring frequently, for 5 minutes, or until softened. Add the beef and cook over high heat, stirring frequently, for 3 minutes, or until browned on all sides and seared.

Add the carrots, then remove from the heat. Gradually stir in the beer and stock, then return to the heat and bring to a boil, stirring. Reduce the heat, then cover and simmer, stirring occasionally, for 1½ hours.

Add the potatoes to the pan and simmer for an additional 15 minutes. Add the bell pepper and corn cobs and simmer for 15 minutes, then add the tomatoes and peas and simmer for an additional 10 minutes, or until the beef and vegetables are tender. Season to taste with salt and pepper, then stir in the cilantro and serve.

SERVES 4

14 oz/400 g lean beef
2 low-salt lean smoked
  Canadian-style bacon
  slices
12 shallots, peeled
1 garlic clove, crushed
8 oz/225 g closed-cap
  mushrooms, sliced

1¼ cups red wine
scant 2 cups beef stock
2 bay leaves
2 tbsp chopped fresh
  thyme
⅓ cup cornstarch
generous ⅓ cup cold
  water

pepper
boiled brown or white
  rice
lightly cooked seasonal
  vegetables

Boeuf Bourguignonne

Trim any visible fat from the beef and cut the beef and bacon into bite-size pieces. Put the meat into a large pan with the shallots, garlic, mushrooms, wine, stock, bay leaves, and 1 tablespoon of the thyme. Bring to a boil, then reduce the heat, cover, and let simmer for 50 minutes, or until the meat and shallots are tender.

Blend the cornstarch with the water in a small bowl and stir into the casserole. Return to a boil, stirring constantly, and cook until the casserole thickens. Reduce the heat and let simmer for an additional 5 minutes. Season to taste with pepper.

Remove and discard the bay leaves. Divide the beef bourguignonne among 4 warmed plates and sprinkle with the remaining thyme. Serve with boiled rice and seasonal vegetables.

SERVES 4

12 oz/350 g fresh lean ground beef
1 large onion, finely chopped
1 tsp dried mixed herbs
1 tbsp all-purpose flour

1¼ cups beef stock
1 tbsp tomato paste
2 large tomatoes, thinly sliced
4 zucchini, thinly sliced
2 tbsp cornstarch

1¼ cups skim milk
⅔ cup ricotta
1 egg yolk
4 tbsp freshly grated Parmesan cheese
salt and pepper

Beef + Tomato Gratin

Preheat the oven to 375°F/190°C. In a large skillet, dry-fry the beef and onion for 4–5 minutes, or until browned.

Stir in the herbs, flour, stock, and tomato paste, and season to taste with salt and pepper. Bring to a boil, then reduce the heat and let simmer for 30 minutes, or until thickened.

Transfer the beef mixture to an ovenproof gratin dish. Cover with a layer of the sliced tomatoes and then add a layer of sliced zucchini. Set aside until required.

Blend the cornstarch with a little of the milk in a small bowl. Pour the remaining milk into a pan and bring to a boil. Add the cornstarch mixture and then cook, stirring, for 1–2 minutes, or until thickened. Remove from the heat and beat in the ricotta and egg yolk. Season well.

Spread the white sauce over the layer of zucchini. Place the dish on a baking sheet and sprinkle with Parmesan cheese. Bake in the oven for 25–30 minutes, or until golden brown. Serve immediately.

SERVES 6

2½ tbsp all-purpose flour
1 tsp salt
¼ tsp pepper
1 rolled brisket of beef, weighing 3 lb 8 oz/ 1.6 kg
2 tbsp vegetable oil

2 tbsp butter
1 onion, finely chopped
2 celery stalks, diced
2 carrots, peeled and diced
1 tsp dill seeds
1 tsp dried thyme or oregano

1½ cups red wine
⅔–1 cup beef stock
4–5 potatoes, cut into large chunks and boiled until just tender
2 tbsp chopped fresh dill, to serve

Pot Roast with Potatoes & Dill

Preheat the oven to 275°F/140°C. Mix 2 tablespoons of the flour with the salt and pepper in a shallow dish. Dip the meat to coat. Heat the oil in a flameproof casserole and brown the meat all over. Transfer to a plate. Add half the butter to the casserole and cook the onion, celery, carrots, dill seeds, and thyme for 5 minutes. Return the meat and juices to the casserole.

Pour in the wine and enough stock to reach one-third of the way up the meat. Bring to a boil, cover, and cook in the oven for 3 hours, turning the meat every 30 minutes. After it has been cooking for 2 hours, add the potatoes and more stock, if necessary.

When ready, transfer the meat and vegetables to a warmed serving dish. Strain the cooking liquid to remove any solids, then return the liquid to the casserole.

Mix the remaining butter and flour to a paste. Bring the cooking liquid to a boil. Whisk in small pieces of the flour-and-butter paste, whisking constantly until the sauce is smooth. Pour the sauce over the meat and vegetables. Sprinkle with the fresh dill to serve.

SERVES 4

- 2 beefsteak tomatoes, cut into thick slices
- 2 red onions, each cut into 6 wedges
- 4 large garlic cloves, peeled
- 1 tsp sea salt
- 3 tbsp olive oil, plus extra for brushing
- 1 heaping tsp dried Herbes de Provence
- 4 lamb chops, about 6 oz/175 g each
- pepper

to serve
- 4 whole wheat pita
- 1/3 cup pine nuts, toasted
- 1 handful fresh basil leaves
- generous 3/4 cup thick plain yogurt

Lamb Chops with Tomatoes

Preheat the oven to 375°F/190°C. Arrange the tomato slices and onion wedges in a roasting pan. Put the garlic cloves and salt in a mortar and crush to a puree with a pestle. Work in the oil. Spoon the mixture over the vegetables and mix well. Sprinkle with the herbs and season to taste with pepper. Put on the top shelf of the preheated oven and roast for 20 minutes.

Meanwhile, lightly brush the lamb chops with oil. Heat a nonstick skillet over high heat. When very hot, add the lamb chops and cook for 1 minute on each side to sear.

Remove the roasting pan from the oven. Turn the vegetables over, then arrange the lamb chops on top and spoon on the juices from the corners of the pan, adding a little water if too dry. Return the pan to the oven and roast for an additional 15–20 minutes, or until the vegetables are tender and the lamb is cooked to your liking. Sprinkle the pita with water and put them in the oven for the last 1–2 minutes of the cooking time.

Scatter the pine nuts and basil over the lamb and vegetables before serving, adding a portion of yogurt and a warmed pita to each plate.

SERVES 4

2 tbsp olive oil
4 lamb shanks, about
    10½ oz/300 g each
2 onions, sliced
2 bell peppers, any color,
    seeded and chopped
2 garlic cloves, well
    crushed

1 eggplant, cut into small
    cubes
½ tsp paprika
½ tsp ground cinnamon
1 cup cooked chickpeas
14 oz/400 g canned
    chopped tomatoes

2 tsp mixed dried
    Mediterranean herbs
scant ½ cup lamb or
    vegetable stock, plus
    extra if needed
salt and pepper
freshly cooked couscous,
    to serve

Turkish Lamb Stew

Preheat the oven to 325°F/160°C. Heat half the oil in a large, nonstick skillet over high heat, then add the lamb shanks and cook, turning frequently, for 2–3 minutes, or until browned all over. Transfer to a casserole dish.

Heat the remaining oil in the skillet over medium-high heat, then add the onions and bell peppers and cook, stirring frequently, for 10–15 minutes, or until the onions are softened and just turning golden. Add the garlic, eggplant, and spices and cook, stirring constantly, for 1 minute. Add the chickpeas, tomatoes and their juice, herbs, and enough stock to cover the bottom of the skillet by about ¾ inch/2 cm, then stir well and bring to a simmer. Season to taste with salt and pepper and transfer to a lidded casserole dish.

Cover the casserole dish with the lid, then transfer to the middle shelf of the preheated oven and cook for 1½ hours. Check after 45 minutes that the casserole is gently bubbling and that there is enough liquid—if it looks dry, add a little more stock or boiling water and stir in. If bubbling too much, reduce the oven temperature. Serve with freshly cooked couscous.

SERVES 4

4 lamb leg steaks
4 tsp ground coriander
1 tbsp ground cumin
1 small butternut squash
1 tbsp olive oil
1 onion, chopped

2½ cups chicken stock
2 tbsp chopped fresh
  ginger
scant ½ cup dried
  apricots
2 tbsp honey

finely grated rind and
  juice of 1 lemon
generous 1 cup
  couscous
salt and pepper
3 tbsp chopped fresh
  mint, to garnish

Honeyed Apricot Lamb with Lemon Couscous

Sprinkle the lamb steaks with the coriander and the cumin, then peel and seed the squash and cut into bite-size chunks.

Heat the oil in a flameproof casserole. Add the lamb and cook over high heat for 2–3 minutes, turning once. Stir in the squash, onion, and half the stock, then bring to a boil.

Add the ginger, apricots, honey, and lemon juice. Season to taste with salt and pepper. Cover and cook over medium heat for about 20 minutes, stirring occasionally.

Meanwhile, bring the remaining stock to a boil in a small saucepan, then stir in the couscous and lemon rind and season to taste with salt and pepper. Remove from the heat, cover, and let stand for 5 minutes. Serve the lamb with the couscous, garnished with mint.

SERVES 4–6

1–2 tbsp olive oil
1 lb/450 g lean boneless lamb
1 onion, finely chopped
2–3 garlic cloves, crushed
5 cups water
14 oz/400 g canned chopped tomatoes
1 bay leaf

½ tsp each dried thyme and oregano
⅛ tsp ground cinnamon
¼ tsp each ground cumin and turmeric
1 tsp harissa, or more to taste
14 oz/400 g canned chickpeas

1 carrot, diced
1 potato, diced
1 zucchini, quartered lengthwise and sliced
⅔ cup fresh or defrosted frozen peas
salt and pepper
sprigs of fresh mint or cilantro, to garnish

Spicy Lamb & Chickpea Stew

Heat 1 tablespoon of the oil in a large saucepan or cast-iron casserole over medium–high heat. Cut the lamb into cubes and add to the pan, in batches if necessary to avoid overcrowding, and cook until evenly browned on all sides, adding a little more oil if needed. Remove the meat with a slotted spoon when browned.

Reduce the heat and add the onion and garlic to the pan. Cook, stirring frequently, for 1–2 minutes.

Add the water and return all the meat to the pan. Bring just to a boil and skim off any foam that rises to the surface. Reduce the heat and stir in the tomatoes, bay leaf, thyme, oregano, cinnamon, cumin, turmeric, and harissa. Simmer for about 1 hour, or until the meat is very tender. Discard the bay leaf.

Rinse and drain the chickpeas, then stir into the pan with the carrot and potato and simmer for 15 minutes. Add the zucchini and peas and continue simmering for 15–20 minutes, or until all the vegetables are tender.

Taste and adjust the seasoning, if necessary, adding more harissa, if desired. Ladle the soup into warmed bowls and serve garnished with mint or cilantro.

SERVES 4

1 lb/450 g lean boneless lamb, such as leg of lamb or tenderloin
1½ tbsp all-purpose flour
1 tsp ground cloves
1–1½ tbsp olive oil
1 white onion, sliced
2–3 garlic cloves, sliced

1¼ cups orange juice
⅔ cup lamb stock or chicken stock
1 cinnamon stick, bruised
2 red bell peppers, seeded and sliced into rings

4 tomatoes
salt and pepper
few fresh sprigs cilantro, plus 1 tbsp chopped fresh cilantro, to garnish

Lamb Stew with Red Bell Peppers

Preheat the oven to 375°F/190°C. Trim any fat or gristle from the lamb and cut into thin strips. Mix the flour and cloves together. Toss the lamb in the spiced flour until well coated and reserve any remaining spiced flour.

Heat 1 tablespoon of the oil in a heavy-bottom skillet and cook the lamb over high heat, stirring frequently, for 3 minutes, or until browned on all sides and sealed. Using a slotted spoon, transfer to an ovenproof casserole.

Add the onion and garlic to the skillet and cook over medium heat, stirring frequently, for 3 minutes, adding the extra oil if necessary. Sprinkle in the reserved spiced flour and cook, stirring constantly, for 2 minutes, then remove from the heat. Gradually stir in the orange juice and stock, then return to the heat and bring to a boil, stirring.

Pour this over the lamb in the casserole, then add the cinnamon stick, red bell peppers, tomatoes, and cilantro sprigs and stir well. Cover and cook in the preheated oven for 1½ hours, or until the lamb is tender.

Discard the cinnamon stick, taste, and adjust the seasoning, if necessary. Serve garnished with the chopped cilantro.

SERVES 4

1¼ cups black-eyed peas, soaked overnight in cold water and drained

3 tbsp sunflower oil

2 lb 4 oz/1 kg boneless leg of lamb, cut into cubes

4 leeks, sliced

1 parsnip, cut into cubes

3 carrots, thickly sliced

2 small turnips, cut into cubes

⅔ cup veal or beef stock

2 tbsp chopped fresh parsley

1 small fresh rosemary sprig

1 tbsp mint jelly

salt and pepper

Lamb & Bean Stew

Put the black-eyed peas into a pan, add cold water to cover, and bring to a boil. Boil vigorously for 15 minutes, then drain and set aside.

Meanwhile, heat the oil in a large skillet. Add the meat and cook over medium heat, stirring frequently, for about 8 minutes, until browned all over. Remove with a slotted spoon and set aside. Add the leeks, parsnip, carrots, and turnips to the skillet and cook, stirring frequently, for about 8 minutes, until softened and beginning to color. Remove with a slotted spoon and set aside. Pour the stock into the skillet, add the parsley, rosemary, and mint jelly, and bring to a boil, scraping up the sediment from the bottom. Remove the skillet from the heat.

Bring a pan of water to a boil. Combine the lamb, vegetables, and peas, season with salt and pepper, and spoon into a 5-cup heatproof bowl. Pour in the stock mixture. Cut a circle of foil 2 inches/5 cm larger than the circumference of the top of the bowl, make a pleat in the center, and put it over the bowl. Tie in place with kitchen twine. Put the bowl into a steamer, cover with a tight-fitting lid, and set it over the pan. Steam for 1¾ hours.

Transfer the lamb, vegetables, and peas to a warm serving dish with a slotted spoon. Remove and discard the rosemary sprig. If the remaining stock mixture is too thin, pour it into a pan and boil until reduced and thickened. Taste and adjust the seasoning, if necessary, and pour it over the stew. Serve immediately.

SERVES 4

all-purpose flour, for coating
1 lb/450 g boneless pork, cut into 1-inch/2.5-cm cubes
1 tbsp vegetable oil
8 oz/225 g chorizo sausage, outer casing removed, cut into bite-size chunks
1 onion, coarsely chopped

4 garlic cloves, finely chopped
2 celery stalks, chopped
1 cinnamon stick, broken
2 bay leaves
2 tsp allspice
2 carrots, sliced
2–3 fresh red chiles, seeded and finely chopped
6 ripe tomatoes, peeled and chopped

4¼ cups pork or vegetable stock
2 sweet potatoes, cut into chunks
corn kernels, cut from 1 ear fresh corn
1 tbsp chopped fresh oregano
salt and pepper
fresh oregano, to garnish

Spicy Pork & Vegetable Stew

Season the flour well with salt and pepper and toss the pork in it to coat. Heat the oil in a large, heavy-bottom pan or ovenproof casserole. Add the chorizo and lightly brown on all sides. Remove the chorizo with a slotted spoon and set aside.

Add the pork, in batches, and cook until browned on all sides. Remove the pork with a slotted spoon and set aside. Add the onion, garlic, and celery to the pan and cook for 5 minutes, or until softened.

Add the cinnamon, bay leaves, and allspice and cook, stirring, for 2 minutes. Add the pork, carrots, chiles, tomatoes, and stock. Bring to a boil, then reduce the heat, cover, and let simmer for 1 hour, or until the pork is tender.

Return the chorizo to the pan with the sweet potatoes, corn, oregano, and season to taste with salt and pepper. Cover and let simmer for an additional 30 minutes, or until the vegetables are tender. Serve garnished with oregano.

SERVES 4

2 tbsp olive oil
1 onion, sliced
1 large yellow bell
    pepper, seeded and
    sliced
1 garlic clove, crushed

1 tsp chile flakes
8 oz/225 g chorizo
    sausage
14 oz/400 g canned
    chopped tomatoes
14 oz/400 g canned
    chickpeas, drained

1 cup basmati rice
handful of arugula leaves
salt and pepper
4 tbsp coarsely chopped
    fresh basil, to garnish

Chorizo, Chile & Chickpea Stew

Heat the oil in a flameproof casserole and fry the onion over medium heat, stirring occasionally, for 5 minutes. Add the bell pepper, garlic, and chile flakes and cook for 2 minutes, stirring.

Chop the chorizo into bite-size chunks and stir into the stew. Add the tomatoes and chickpeas and season to taste with salt and pepper. Bring to a boil, cover, and simmer for 10 minutes.

Meanwhile, cook the rice in a saucepan of lightly salted boiling water for 10–12 minutes, until tender. Drain. Stir the arugula into the stew. Serve spooned over the rice, garnished with basil.

SERVES 4

1–1 lb 4 oz/450–550 g lean ham
1–2 tbsp olive oil, plus 1–2 tsp extra
1 onion, chopped
2–3 garlic cloves, chopped
2 celery stalks, chopped
6 carrots, sliced
1 cinnamon stick, bruised
½ tsp ground cloves
¼ tsp freshly grated nutmeg
1 tsp dried oregano
scant 2 cups chicken stock or vegetable stock
1–2 tbsp maple syrup
3 large, spicy sausages, about 8 oz/225 g, or chorizo (outer casing removed)
14 oz/400 g canned black-eyed peas or fava beans
1 orange bell pepper
1 tbsp cornstarch
pepper

Ham with Black-Eyed Peas

Trim off any fat or skin from the ham and cut into 1½-inch/4-cm chunks. Heat 1 tablespoon of oil in a heavy-bottom pan and cook the ham over high heat, stirring frequently, for 5 minutes, or until browned on all sides and sealed. Using a slotted spoon, remove from the pan and set aside.

Add the onion, garlic, celery, and carrots to the pan with an additional tablespoon of oil, if necessary, and cook over a medium heat, stirring frequently, for 5 minutes, or until softened. Add all the spices and season to taste with pepper, then cook, stirring constantly, for 2 minutes.

Return the ham to the pan. Add the dried oregano, stock, and maple syrup to taste, then bring to a boil, stirring. Reduce the heat, then cover and simmer, stirring occasionally, for 1 hour.

Heat the remaining 1–2 teaspoons of oil in a skillet and cook the sausages, turning frequently, until browned all over. Remove and cut each into 3–4 chunks, then add to the pan. Drain and rinse the peas, then drain again. Seed and chop the bell pepper. Add the beans and bell pepper to the pan, and simmer for an additional 20 minutes. Blend 2 tablespoons of water with the cornstarch and stir into the stew, then cook for 3–5 minutes. Discard the cinnamon stick and serve.

SERVES 4

1 lb/450 g lean boneless pork
1½ tbsp all-purpose flour
1 tsp ground coriander
1 tsp ground cumin
1½ tsp ground cinnamon
1 tbsp olive oil

1 onion, chopped
14 oz/400 g canned chopped tomatoes
2 tbsp tomato paste
2 cups chicken stock
4 carrots, chopped
3 cups chopped squash, such as kabocha

2½ cups sliced leeks, blanched and drained
4 oz/115 g okra, trimmed and sliced
salt and pepper
sprigs of fresh parsley, to garnish
couscous, to serve

Pork & Vegetable Stew

Trim off any fat or gristle from the pork and cut into thin strips about 2-inches/5-cm long. Mix the flour and spices together. Toss the pork in the spiced flour until well coated and reserve any remaining spiced flour.

Heat the oil in a large, heavy-bottom pan and cook the onion, stirring frequently, for 5 minutes, or until softened. Add the pork and cook over high heat, stirring frequently, for 5 minutes, or until browned on all sides and sealed. Sprinkle in the reserved spiced flour and cook, stirring constantly, for 2 minutes, then remove from the heat.

Gradually add the tomatoes to the pan. Blend the tomato paste with a little of the stock in a pitcher and gradually stir into the pan, then stir in half the remaining stock.

Add the carrots, then return to the heat and bring to a boil, stirring. Reduce the heat, then cover and simmer, stirring occasionally, for 1½ hours. Add the squash and cook for an additional 15 minutes.

Add the leeks and okra and the remaining stock if you prefer a thinner stew. Simmer for an additional 15 minutes, or until the pork and vegetables are tender. Season to taste with salt and pepper, then garnish with fresh parsley and serve with couscous.

SERVES 4

12 oz/350 g lean pork tenderloin
1 tbsp vegetable oil
1 medium onion, chopped
2 garlic cloves, crushed
2 tbsp all-purpose flour

2 tbsp tomato paste
generous 1¾ cups chicken or vegetable stock
1¾ cups sliced button mushrooms
1 large green bell pepper, seeded

½ tsp freshly grated nutmeg, plus extra to garnish
salt and pepper
boiled rice with chopped fresh parsley, to serve
4 tbsp lowfat plain yogurt

Pork Stroganoff

Trim away any excess fat and silver skin from the pork, then cut the meat into ½-inch/1-cm thick slices. Heat the vegetable oil in a large, heavy-bottom skillet and gently cook the pork, onion, and garlic for 4–5 minutes, or until lightly browned.

Stir in the flour and tomato paste, then pour in the chicken stock and stir to mix thoroughly. Add the mushrooms, bell pepper, nutmeg, and season to taste with salt and pepper. Bring to a boil, cover, and let simmer for 20 minutes, or until the pork is tender and cooked through.

Remove the skillet from the heat. Transfer the pork to 4 large, warmed serving plates and serve with boiled rice sprinkled with fresh parsley and a spoonful of yogurt, garnished with freshly grated nutmeg.

SERVES 4

8 skinless, boneless chicken thighs, about 3½ oz/100 g each
2 tbsp sweet chili dipping sauce
2 tbsp orange juice
2 garlic cloves, well crushed
salt and pepper

creole rice

2½ cups water
1¼ cups white long-grain rice
1 tbsp olive oil
1 large red bell pepper, seeded and finely chopped
1 small onion, finely chopped
1 tsp paprika
14 oz/400 g canned mixed beans, drained and rinsed

Sweet Chili Chicken with Creole Rice

Put the chicken in a shallow, nonmetallic bowl. Mix the chili sauce, orange juice, and garlic in a small bowl, spoon over the chicken, and season with salt and pepper. Using your hands, coat the chicken thighs thoroughly in the marinade. Cover and let marinate in the refrigerator for 1–2 hours.

Preheat the oven to 350°F/180°C. Transfer the chicken thighs to a nonstick baking sheet and bake in the preheated oven, turning halfway through, for 25 minutes, or until tender and the juices run clear when a skewer is inserted into the thickest part of the meat.

Meanwhile, make the rice. Lightly salt the water and bring to a boil in a saucepan. Add the rice and stir well. Cover, then reduce the heat to low and let simmer, undisturbed, for 15 minutes, or until tender and all the water has been absorbed.

While the rice is cooking, heat the oil in a nonstick skillet over medium–high heat. Add the bell pepper and onion and cook, stirring frequently, for 10–15 minutes, or until the onion is thoroughly soft and turning golden, adding the paprika for the last 5 minutes of the cooking time. Stir in the beans and cook for an additional 1 minute.

Stir the bean mixture into the rice, then serve immediately with the baked chicken.

SERVES 4

4 skinless, boneless
chicken breasts
4 tbsp green olive
tapenade

8 thin slices smoked
pancetta
2 garlic cloves, coarsely
chopped
1¾ cups halved cherry
tomatoes

scant ½ cup dry white
wine
2 tbsp olive oil
8 slices ciabatta
salt and pepper

Baked Tapenade Chicken

Preheat the oven to 425°F/220°C. Put the chicken breasts on a cutting board and cut three deep slashes into each. Spread a tablespoon of the tapenade over each chicken breast, pushing it into the slashes with a palette knife.

Wrap each chicken breast in two slices of pancetta. Place the chicken breasts in a shallow ovenproof dish and arrange the garlic and tomatoes around them. Season to taste with salt and pepper, then pour the wine and 1 tablespoon of the oil on top. Bake in the preheated oven for about 20 minutes, until the juices run clear when the chicken is pierced with a skewer. Cover the dish loosely with aluminum foil and let stand for 5 minutes.

Meanwhile, preheat the broiler to high. Brush the ciabatta with the remaining oil and cook under the preheated broiler for 2–3 minutes, turning once, until golden. Serve the chicken with the golden ciabatta.

SERVES 4

2 tbsp butter
8 pearl onions
4½ oz/125 g lean bacon, coarsely chopped
4 fresh chicken pieces

1 garlic clove, finely chopped
12 white mushrooms
1¼ cups red wine
1 bouquet garni

1 tbsp chopped fresh tarragon
salt and pepper
2 tsp cornstarch
chopped fresh flat-leaf parsley, to garnish

Coq Au Vin

Melt half of the butter in a large skillet over medium heat. Add the onions and bacon and cook, stirring, for 3 minutes. Lift out the bacon and onions and set aside. Melt the remaining butter in the pan and add the chicken. Cook for 3 minutes, then turn over and cook on the other side for 2 minutes.

Drain off any excess chicken fat. Return the bacon and onions to the pan, then add the garlic, mushrooms, red wine, and herbs. Season to taste with salt and pepper. Cook for about 1 hour, or until cooked through. Remove from the heat, lift out the chicken, onions, bacon, and mushrooms, transfer them to a serving platter, and keep warm. Discard the bouquet garni.

Mix the cornstarch with 1–2 tablespoons of water, then stir it into the juices in the pan. Bring to a boil, lower the heat, and cook, stirring, for 1 minute. Pour the sauce over the chicken and serve, garnished with parsley.

SERVES 4

3 tbsp olive oil
5 lb/2.5 kg chicken,
  cut into 8 pieces and
  dusted with flour
7 oz/200 g fresh chorizo
  sausages, thickly sliced
a small bunch of fresh
  sage leaves

1 onion, chopped
6 garlic cloves, sliced
2 celery stalks, sliced
1 small pumpkin or
  butternut squash,
  peeled and roughly
  chopped
1 cup dry sherry

2½ cups chicken stock
14 oz/400 g canned
  chopped tomatoes
2 bay leaves
salt and pepper
a small bunch of fresh
  flat-leaf parsley,
  chopped

Chicken, Pumpkin & Chorizo Stew

Preheat the oven to 350°F/180°C. Heat the oil in a casserole dish and fry the chicken with the chorizo and sage leaves until golden brown. Remove with a slotted spoon and reserve. You may need to do this in two batches.

Add the onion, garlic, celery, and pumpkin and cook until the mixture begins to brown slightly. Add the sherry, chicken stock, tomatoes, and bay leaves and season to taste with salt and pepper. Return the reserved chicken, chorizo, and sage to the casserole, cover, and cook in the oven for 1 hour.

Remove the stew from the oven, uncover, then remove the bay leaves. Stir in the chopped parsley and serve.

SERVES 4

4 lb/1.8 kg chicken pieces
2 tbsp sunflower oil
2 medium leeks
4 carrots, chopped
2 parsnips, chopped

2 small turnips, chopped
2½ cups chicken stock
3 tbsp Worcestershire sauce
2 sprigs fresh rosemary
salt and pepper

dumplings
1⅔ cups self-rising flour
½ cup lard
1 tbsp chopped rosemary leaves
cold water, to mix

Chicken Stew with Dumplings

Remove the skin from the chicken, if you prefer. Heat the oil in a large, flameproof casserole or heavy-bottom pan and fry the chicken until golden. Using a slotted spoon, remove the chicken from the pan. Drain off the excess fat.

Trim and slice the leeks. Add the carrots, parsnips, and turnips to the casserole and cook for 5 minutes, until lightly colored. Return the chicken to the pan. Add the chicken stock, Worcestershire sauce, and rosemary, season to taste with salt and pepper, then bring to a boil. Reduce the heat, cover, and simmer gently for about 50 minutes, or until the juices run clear when the chicken is pierced with a skewer.

To make the dumplings, combine the flour, lard, and rosemary in a bowl and season with salt and pepper. Stir in just enough cold water to bind to a firm dough. Form into 8 small balls and place on top of the chicken and vegetables. Cover and simmer for an additional 10–12 minutes, until the dumplings are well risen. Serve with the stew.

SERVES 4

4 tbsp sunflower oil
2 lb/900 g chicken meat, chopped
3 cups white mushrooms, sliced
16 shallots
6 garlic cloves, chopped finely

1 tbsp all-purpose flour
1 cup white wine
1 cup chicken bouillon
1 fresh bouquet garni, with sage and 1 celery stalk

14 oz/400 g canned borlotti beans, drained and rinsed
salt and pepper
steamed squash, to serve

Garlic Chicken Stew

Preheat the oven to 300°F/150°C. Heat the sunflower oil in an ovenproof casserole and sauté the chicken until browned all over. Remove the chicken from the casserole with a slotted spoon and set aside until required. Add the mushrooms, shallots, and garlic to the casserole and cook for 4 minutes.

Return the chicken to the casserole and sprinkle with the flour, then cook for another 2 minutes. Add the white wine and chicken bouillon, stir until boiling, then add the bouquet garni. Season to taste with salt and pepper. Add the beans to the casserole.

Cover and place in the center of the preheated oven for 2 hours. Remove the bouquet garni and serve the casserole with the squash.

SERVES 4

6 tbsp all-purpose flour
4 turkey breast fillets
3 tbsp corn oil
1 onion, thinly sliced
1 red bell pepper, seeded and sliced
1¼ cups chicken stock
2 tbsp raisins
4 tomatoes, peeled, seeded, and chopped
1 tsp chili powder
½ tsp ground cinnamon
pinch of ground cumin
1 oz/25 g semisweet chocolate, finely chopped or grated
salt and pepper
sprigs of fresh cilantro, to garnish

Spiced Turkey

Preheat the oven to 325°F/160°C. Spread the flour on a plate and season with salt and pepper. Coat the turkey fillets in the seasoned flour, shaking off any excess.

Heat the oil in a flameproof casserole. Add the turkey fillets and cook over medium heat, turning occasionally, for 5–10 minutes, or until golden. Transfer to a plate with a slotted spoon.

Add the onion and bell pepper to the casserole. Cook over low heat, stirring occasionally, for 5 minutes, or until softened. Sprinkle in any remaining seasoned flour and cook, stirring constantly, for 1 minute. Gradually stir in the stock, then add the raisins, chopped tomatoes, chili powder, cinnamon, cumin, and chocolate. Season to taste with salt and pepper. Bring to a boil, stirring constantly.

Return the turkey to the casserole, cover, and cook in the preheated oven for 50 minutes. Serve immediately, garnished with sprigs of cilantro.

SERVES 4

4 duck breasts, about
  5½ oz/150 g each
2 tbsp olive oil
8 oz/225 g piece ham,
  cut into small chunks
8 oz/225 g chorizo, outer
  casing removed, cut
  into chunks
1 onion, chopped

3 garlic cloves, chopped
3 celery stalks, chopped
1–2 fresh red chiles,
  seeded and chopped
1 green bell pepper,
  seeded and chopped
2½ cups chicken stock
1 tbsp chopped fresh
  oregano

14 oz/400 g canned
  chopped tomatoes
1–2 tsp hot pepper
  sauce, or to taste
chopped fresh parsley,
  to garnish
salad greens and freshly
  cooked long-grain rice,
  to serve

Duck Jambalaya-Style Stew

Remove and discard the skin and any fat from the duck breasts. Cut the flesh into bite-size pieces.

Heat half the oil in a large, deep skillet and cook the duck, ham, and chorizo over high heat, stirring frequently, for 5 minutes, or until browned on all sides and seared. Using a slotted spoon, remove from the skillet and set aside.

Add the onion, garlic, celery, and chiles to the skillet and cook over medium heat, stirring frequently, for 5 minutes, or until softened. Add the bell pepper, then stir in the stock, oregano, tomatoes, and hot pepper sauce.

Bring to a boil, then reduce the heat and return the duck, ham, and chorizo to the skillet. Cover and simmer, stirring occasionally, for 20 minutes, or until the duck and ham are tender.

Serve immediately, garnished with parsley and accompanied by salad greens and rice.

Fish & Seafood

SERVES 4

8 monkfish fillets, weighing about 1 lb 12 oz/800 g in total
6 tbsp olive oil
1 onion, halved and thinly sliced into crescents
½ tsp finely chopped fresh rosemary
1 fresh red chile, halved, seeded, and thinly sliced
3 tbsp capers, drained and rinsed
1 tbsp chopped flat-leaf parsley
coarsely grated zest of ½ lemon
1 cup dry white wine
pat of butter
4 thin slices ciabatta or sourdough bread
salt and pepper

Baked Monkfish with Toasted Ciabatta

Preheat the oven to 400°F/200°C. Remove any membrane from the monkfish fillets. Sprinkle with ½ teaspoon of salt and ¼ teaspoon of pepper.

Heat 4 tablespoons of the olive oil in a flameproof gratin dish. Add the onion and rosemary and cook over medium heat for 5 minutes, until the onion is softened but not colored. Add the chile, capers, parsley, and lemon zest and cook for another 3 minutes, until the onion is just beginning to color. Pour in the wine, bring to a boil, and simmer for 1 minute.

Remove the dish from the heat. Add the monkfish fillets in a single layer, spooning some of the onion mixture over the top. Cook in the oven for 20–25 minutes, until the thickest part of the flesh looks opaque when pierced with the tip of a knife.

Transfer the fillets to a plate and keep warm. Bring the contents of the dish to a boil, and simmer over medium–high heat for 2–3 minutes, until the liquid is slightly reduced. Swirl in a pat of butter, then taste and adjust the seasoning, if necessary.

Heat the remaining 2 tablespoons of olive oil in a skillet. Add the slices of bread and pan-fry for 1–2 minutes, until golden on both sides.

Place a slice of bread on each serving plate. Arrange the monkfish fillets on top and spoon the sauce over them.

SERVES 8

2 lb 4 oz/1 kg selection of at least 4 different firm white fish fillets, such as red snapper, sea bass, eel, or monkfish, scaled and cleaned, but not skinned
generous ⅓ cup olive oil
2 onions, finely chopped
1 fennel bulb, finely chopped

4 garlic cloves, crushed
2 lb 6 oz/1.2 kg canned chopped plum tomatoes
6 cups fish stock
pinch of saffron strands
grated zest of 1 orange
bouquet garni of 2 sprigs thyme, 2 sprigs parsley, and 2 bay leaves, tied together with kitchen twine

1 lb 2 oz/500 g mussels, cleaned
1 lb 2 oz/500 g cooked shrimp, shell on
salt and pepper
crusty French baguette and rouille, to serve

Bouillabaisse

Carefully pin bone the fish, then cut the fillets into bite-size pieces.

Heat the olive oil in a very large skillet or wide saucepan with a lid and gently fry the onion and fennel for about 15 minutes, until softened. Add the garlic and fry for 2 minutes, then add the tomatoes and simmer for 2 minutes. Add the stock, saffron, orange zest, and bouquet garni and bring to a boil. Simmer, uncovered, for 15 minutes.

Add the fish pieces, mussels, and shrimp and cover the skillet. Simmer for an additional 5–10 minutes, until the mussels have opened. Discard any that remain closed. Taste and adjust the seasoning, if necessary.

Serve with some crusty baguette and rouille.

SERVES 6

butter, for greasing
2 lb/900 g white fish
  fillets, such as flounder,
  skinned
2/3 cup dry white wine
1 tbsp chopped fresh
  parsley, tarragon, or dill

2½ cups sliced small
  mushrooms
7 tbsp butter
6 oz/175 g cooked
  shelled shrimp
1/3 cup all-purpose flour
½ cup heavy cream

2 lb/900 g starchy
  potatoes, peeled and
  cut into even-size
  chunks
salt and pepper

Fisherman's Pie

Preheat the oven to 350°F/180°C. Butter a 2-quart/1.7-liter ovenproof dish. Fold the fish fillets in half and place in the dish. Season to taste with salt and pepper, pour the wine and scatter the herbs on top. Cover with foil and bake for 15 minutes, until the fish starts to flake. Strain off the liquid and reserve for the sauce. Increase the oven temperature to 425°F/220°C. Sauté the mushrooms in a skillet with 1 tablespoon of the butter and spoon over the fish. Scatter the shrimp on top.

Heat 4 tablespoons of the butter in a saucepan and stir in the flour. Cook for a few minutes without browning, remove from the heat, then add the reserved cooking liquid gradually, stirring well between each addition. Return to the heat and gently bring to a boil, still stirring to ensure a smooth sauce. Add the cream and season to taste with salt and pepper. Pour over the fish in the dish and smooth over the surface.

Make mashed potatoes by cooking the potatoes in boiling salted water for 15–20 minutes. Drain well and mash with a potato masher until smooth. Season to taste with salt and pepper and add the remaining butter, stirring until melted. Pile or pipe the potatoes onto the fish and sauce and bake for 10–15 minutes, until golden brown. Serve immediately.

SERVES 4

7 oz/200 g squid, cleaned and tentacles discarded

1 lb 2 oz/500 g firm whitefish fillets

1 tbsp corn oil

4 shallots, finely chopped

2 garlic cloves, finely chopped

2 tbsp Thai green curry paste

2 small lemongrass stalks, finely chopped

1 tsp shrimp paste

generous 2 cups coconut milk

7 oz/200 g jumbo shrimp, peeled and deveined

12 clams, scrubbed

8 fresh basil leaves, finely shredded, plus extra leaves to garnish

freshly cooked rice, to serve

Spicy Thai Seafood Stew

Using a sharp knife, cut the squid into thick rings and cut the fish into bite-size chunks.

Preheat a large wok, then add the oil and heat. Add the shallots, garlic, and curry paste and stir-fry for 1–2 minutes. Add the lemongrass and shrimp paste, then stir in the coconut milk and bring to a boil.

Reduce the heat until the liquid is simmering gently, then add the squid, fish, and shrimp and simmer for 2 minutes.

Discard any clams with broken shells and any that refuse to close when tapped. Add the clams to the wok and simmer for an additional minute, or until the clams have opened. Discard any that remain closed. Sprinkle the shredded basil leaves over the stew.

Transfer to serving plates, garnish with basil leaves, and serve immediately with freshly cooked rice.

SERVES 4

10 oz/285 g prepared
  squid
3 tbsp olive oil
1 onion, chopped
3 garlic cloves, finely
  chopped

1 tsp fresh thyme leaves
14 oz/400 g canned
  chopped tomatoes
⅔ cup red wine
1¼ cups water

1 tbsp chopped fresh
  parsley
salt and pepper
crusty bread, to serve

Squid Stew

Preheat the oven to 275°F/140°C. Rinse the squid along with the tentacles under running water. Slice the body into rings. Drain well on paper towels. Heat the oil in a large, flameproof casserole. Add the prepared squid and cook over medium heat, stirring occasionally, until lightly browned.

Reduce the heat and add the onion, garlic, and thyme. Cook for an additional 5 minutes, until softened.

Stir in the tomatoes, red wine, and water. Bring to a boil, then transfer to the preheated oven and cook for 2 hours. Season to taste with salt and pepper. Divide among 4 bowls, sprinkle with the parsley, and serve with the crusty bread.

SERVES 4

1 yellow bell pepper,
1 red bell pepper,
1 orange bell pepper,
seeded and cut into
quarters
4 ripe tomatoes
2 large, fresh, mild green
chiles, such as poblano
6 garlic cloves
2 tsp dried oregano or
dried mixed herbs

2 tbsp olive oil, plus extra
for drizzling
1 large onion, finely
chopped
scant 2 cups fish,
vegetable, or chicken
stock
finely grated rind and
juice of 1 lime
2 tbsp chopped fresh
cilantro, plus extra
to garnish

1 bay leaf
1 lb/450 g red snapper
fillets, skinned and cut
into chunks
8 oz/225 g raw shrimp,
shelled and deveined
8 oz/225 g raw squid
rings
salt and pepper
warmed flour tortillas,
to serve

Southwestern Seafood Stew

Preheat the oven to 400°F/200°C. Put the bell pepper quarters, skin-side up, in a roasting pan with the tomatoes, chiles, and garlic. Sprinkle with the oregano and drizzle with oil. Roast in the preheated oven for 30 minutes, or until the bell peppers are well browned and softened.

Remove the roasted vegetables from the oven and let stand until cool enough to handle. Peel and finely chop the garlic.

Heat the oil in a large pan and cook the onion, stirring frequently, for 5 minutes, or until softened. Add the bell peppers, tomatoes, chiles, garlic, stock, lime rind and juice, cilantro, and bay leaf and season to taste with salt and pepper. Bring to a boil, then stir in the fish and seafood. Reduce the heat, then cover and simmer gently for 10 minutes, or until the fish and squid are just cooked through and the shrimp have turned pink. Discard the bay leaf, then garnish with chopped cilantro before serving, accompanied by warmed flour tortillas.

SERVES 4

2 tbsp olive oil
2 red onions, finely
  chopped
1 garlic clove, crushed
2 zucchini, sliced
14 oz/400 g canned
  chopped tomatoes

3¾ cups fish stock or
  vegetable stock
¾ cup dried pasta
  shapes
12 oz/350 g firm whitefish,
  such as flounder,
  swordfish, or halibut

1 tbsp chopped fresh
  basil, plus extra sprigs
  to garnish
1 tsp grated lemon rind
1 tbsp cornstarch
1 tbsp water
salt and pepper

Italian Fish Stew

Heat the oil in a large pan. Add the onions and garlic and cook over low heat, stirring occasionally, for about 5 minutes, until softened. Add the zucchini and cook, stirring frequently, for 2–3 minutes.

Add the tomatoes and stock to the pan and bring to a boil. Add the pasta, bring back to a boil, reduce the heat, and cover. Simmer for 5 minutes.

Skin and bone the fish, then cut it into chunks. Add to the pan with the basil and lemon rind and simmer gently for 5 minutes, until the fish is opaque and flakes easily (be careful to avoid overcooking it) and the pasta is tender, but still firm to the bite.

Place the cornstarch and water in a small bowl, mix to a smooth paste, and stir into the stew. Cook gently for 2 minutes, stirring constantly, until thickened. Season to taste with salt and pepper.

Ladle the stew into 4 warmed bowls. Garnish with basil and serve immediately.

SERVES 4

2 tsp butter
1 large leek, thinly sliced
2 shallots, finely chopped
½ cup hard cider
1¼ cups fish stock
2 potatoes, diced

1 bay leaf
4 tbsp all-purpose flour
¾ cup milk
¾ cup heavy cream
1¾ cups chopped fresh
  sorrel leaves

12 oz/350 g skinless
  striped bass or halibut,
  cut into 1-inch/2.5-cm
  pieces
salt and pepper

Fish Stew with Cider

Melt the butter in a large saucepan over medium–low heat. Add the leek and shallots and cook for about 5 minutes, stirring frequently, until they start to soften. Add the cider and bring to a boil.

Stir in the stock, potatoes, and bay leaf with a large pinch of salt (unless the stock is salty) and bring back to a boil. Reduce the heat, cover, and cook gently for 10 minutes.

Put the flour in a small bowl and very slowly whisk in a few tablespoons of the milk to make a thick paste. Stir in a little more to make a smooth liquid.

Adjust the heat so the soup bubbles gently. Stir in the flour mixture and cook, stirring frequently, for 5 minutes. Add the remaining milk and half the cream. Continue cooking for about 10 minutes, until the potatoes are tender.

Combine the sorrel with the remaining cream. Stir the sorrel cream into the stew and add the fish. Continue cooking, stirring occasionally, for about 3 minutes, until the monkfish stiffens or the cod just begins to flake. Taste and adjust the seasoning, if necessary. Ladle into warmed bowls, remove the bay leaf, and serve.

SERVES 4-6

large pinch of saffron
  threads
4 tbsp almost-boiling
  water
6 tbsp olive oil
1 large onion, chopped
2 garlic cloves, finely
  chopped
1½ tbsp chopped fresh
  thyme leaves
2 bay leaves

2 red bell peppers,
  seeded and roughly
  chopped
1 lb 12 oz/800 g canned
  chopped tomatoes
1 tsp smoked paprika
9 fl oz/250 ml fish stock
5 oz/140 g blanched
  almonds, toasted and
  finely ground
12-16 mussels
12-16 clams

1 lb 5 oz/600 g thick,
  boned and skinned
  fillets of striped bass,
  halibut, or monkfish,
  cut into 2-inch/5-cm
  chunks
12-16 shrimp, shelled
  and deveined
salt and pepper
thick crusty bread,
  to serve

Catalan Fish Stew

Put the saffron threads in a heatproof pitcher with the water and let stand for at least 10 minutes to steep.

Heat the oil in a large, flameproof casserole over medium–high heat. Reduce the heat to low and cook the onion, stirring occasionally, for 10 minutes, or until golden but not browned. Stir in the garlic, thyme, bay leaves, and bell peppers and cook, stirring frequently, for 5 minutes, or until the bell peppers are softened and the onions have softened further. Add the tomatoes and paprika and simmer, stirring frequently, for an additional 5 minutes.

Stir in the stock, the saffron and its soaking liquid, and the almonds and bring to a boil, stirring. Reduce the heat and simmer for 5–10 minutes, until the sauce reduces and thickens. Season to taste with salt and pepper.

Meanwhile, clean the mussels and clams by scrubbing or scraping the shells and pulling out any beards that are attached to the mussels. Discard any with broken shells or any that refuse to close when tapped.

Gently stir the fish chunks into the stew so that they don't break up, then add the shrimp, mussels, and clams. Reduce the heat to very low, cover, and simmer for 5 minutes, or until the fish is opaque, the mussels and clams have opened, and the shrimp have turned pink. Discard any mussels or clams that remain closed. Serve immediately with plenty of thick crusty bread for soaking up.

SERVES 4-6

7 oz/200 g dried egg ribbon pasta, such as tagliatelle
2 tbsp butter
1 cup fine fresh breadcrumbs
1¾ cups condensed canned cream of mushroom soup

½ cup milk
2 celery stalks, chopped
1 red and 1 green bell pepper, cored, seeded, and chopped
1¼ cups shredded sharp cheddar cheese

2 tbsp chopped fresh parsley
7 oz/200 g canned tuna in oil, drained and flaked
salt and pepper

Tuna-Noodle Stew

Preheat the oven to 400°F/200°C. Bring a large pan of salted water to a boil. Add the pasta and cook for 2 minutes less than specified on the package instructions.

Meanwhile, melt the butter in a separate, small pan over medium heat. Stir in the breadcrumbs, then remove from the heat and set aside.

Drain the pasta well and set aside. Pour the soup into the pasta pan over medium heat, then stir in the milk, celery, bell peppers, half the cheese, and the parsley. Add the tuna and gently stir in so that the flakes don't break up. Season to taste with salt and pepper. Heat just until small bubbles appear around the edge of the mixture but do not boil.

Stir the pasta into the pan and use 2 forks to mix all the ingredients together. Spoon the mixture into an ovenproof dish that is also suitable for serving and spread out.

Stir the remaining cheese into the buttered breadcrumbs, then sprinkle over the top of the pasta mixture. Bake in the oven for 20–25 minutes, until the topping is golden. Let stand for 5 minutes before serving straight from the dish.

SERVES 4

2 tbsp butter, plus extra
  for greasing
1 lb/450 g smoked
  flounder or halibut, cut
  into 4 portions
2½ cups milk
scant ¼ cup all-purpose
  flour

pinch of freshly grated
  nutmeg
3 tbsp heavy cream
1 tbsp chopped fresh
  parsley
2 eggs, hard-cooked and
  mashed to a pulp

1 lb/450 g dried fusilli
  pasta
1 tbsp lemon juice
salt and pepper
fresh flat-leaf parsley,
  to garnish

Smoked Fish Casserole

Preheat the oven to 400°F/200°C. Generously grease a casserole with butter. Put the smoked fish in the casserole and pour in the milk. Bake in the preheated oven for about 15 minutes, until tender and the flesh flakes easily.

Carefully pour the cooking liquid into a pitcher without breaking up the fish and reserve. The fish should remain in the casserole.

Melt the butter in a pan and stir in the flour. Gradually whisk in the cooking liquid. Season to taste with salt, pepper, and nutmeg. Stir in the cream, chopped parsley, and mashed eggs and cook, stirring, for 2 minutes.

Meanwhile, bring a large pan of lightly salted water to a boil. Add the fusilli and lemon juice, bring back to a boil, and cook for 8–10 minutes, until tender but still firm to the bite.

Drain the pasta and spoon or turn it over the fish. Top with the egg sauce and return the casserole to the oven for 10 minutes.

Transfer the smoked fish casserole to serving plates. Serve piping hot, garnished with flat-leaf parsley.

SERVES 4

2 tbsp olive oil
2 large onions, sliced into rings
3 garlic cloves, chopped

2 large zucchini, cut into sticks
3 tbsp fresh thyme, stalks removed
8 large sardine fillets

1 cup grated Parmesan cheese
4 eggs, beaten
2/3 cup milk
salt and pepper

Fresh Baked Sardines

Preheat the oven to 350°F/180°C. Heat 1 tablespoon of the olive oil in a skillet. Add the onion rings and chopped garlic and fry over low heat, stirring occasionally, for 2–3 minutes. Add the zucchini to the skillet and cook, stirring occasionally, for about 5 minutes, or until golden. Stir in 2 tablespoons of the thyme.

Place half the onions and zucchini in the bottom of a large ovenproof dish. Top with the sardine fillets and half the grated Parmesan cheese. Place the remaining onions and zucchini on top and sprinkle with the remaining thyme.

Combine the eggs and milk in a bowl and season to taste with salt and pepper. Pour the mixture over the vegetables and sardines in the dish. Sprinkle the remaining Parmesan cheese over the top. Bake for 20–25 minutes, or until golden and set. Serve immediately.

SERVES 4

2 tbsp olive oil
12 scallops, shelled, cleaned, and halved
1 large onion, finely chopped
2 garlic cloves, well crushed
14 oz/400 g canned chopped tomatoes

2 tsp dried Herbes de Provence
⅔ cup dry white wine
1 mild red chile, seeded and chopped (optional)
5 oz/150 g cooked shelled mussels

7 oz/200 g large cooked, peeled jumbo shrimp
pepper
2 tbsp chopped fresh parsley, for serving

Seafood Provençale

Heat the oil in a large skillet over high heat, then add the scallops and cook for 30 seconds on each side to sear. Remove with a spatula and set aside.

Reduce the heat to medium, then add the onion and cook for 8–10 minutes, or until softened and just turning golden. Add the garlic and cook, stirring, for 1 minute, then add the tomatoes and their juice, herbs, wine, chile, if using, and season to taste with pepper. Bring to a simmer and cook for 20 minutes.

Add the mussels and shrimp to the skillet with the scallops and gently simmer for an additional 5 minutes. Serve immediately, sprinkled with the parsley.

SERVES 4–6

12 oz/350 g mussels, scrubbed and debearded
4 tbsp olive oil
1 onion, finely chopped
1 green bell pepper, seeded and chopped
2 garlic cloves, very finely chopped
5 tbsp tomato paste

1 tbsp chopped fresh flat-leaf parsley
1 tsp dried oregano
14 oz/400 g canned chopped tomatoes
1 cup dry red wine
1 lb/450 g firm whitefish, such as cod or monkfish, cut into 2-inch/5-cm pieces

4 oz/115 g scallops, halved
4 oz/115 g shrimp, peeled and deveined
7 oz/200 g canned crabmeat
salt and pepper
10–15 fresh basil leaves, shredded, to garnish

Seafood Stew with Red Wine & Tomatoes

Discard any mussels with broken shells and any that refuse to close when tapped.

Heat the oil in a large, heavy-bottom pan or flameproof casserole over medium heat. Add the onion and bell pepper and cook for 5 minutes, or until beginning to soften. Stir in the garlic, tomato paste, parsley, and oregano and cook for 1 minute, stirring. Pour in the tomatoes and wine. Season to taste with salt and pepper. Bring to a boil, then cover and simmer over low heat for 30 minutes.

Add the fish, cover, and simmer for 15 minutes. Add the mussels, scallops, shrimp, and crabmeat. Cover and cook for an additional 15 minutes. Discard any mussels that remain closed. Stir in the basil just before serving.

SERVES 4

2 tbsp olive oil
1 onion, finely chopped
1 celery stalk, finely
   chopped

1 cup pitted green olives
4 tomatoes, chopped
3 tbsp bottled capers,
   drained

4 swordfish steaks, about
   5 oz/140 g each
salt and pepper
fresh flat-leaf parsley
   sprigs, to garnish

Mediterranean Swordfish

Heat the oil in a large, heavy-bottom skillet. Add the onion and celery, and cook over low heat, stirring occasionally, for 5 minutes, or until softened.

Meanwhile, roughly chop half the olives. Stir the chopped and whole olives into the skillet with the tomatoes and capers, and season to taste with salt and pepper.

Bring to a boil, then reduce the heat, cover, and simmer gently, stirring occasionally, for 15 minutes.

Add the swordfish steaks to the skillet and return to a boil. Cover and simmer, turning the fish once, for 20 minutes, or until the fish is cooked and the flesh flakes easily. Transfer the fish to serving plates and spoon the sauce over them. Garnish with fresh parsley sprigs and serve immediately.

SERVES 4

2 tbsp olive oil
1 large onion, finely
   chopped
pinch of saffron threads
½ tsp ground cinnamon
1 tsp ground coriander
½ tsp ground cumin

½ tsp ground turmeric
7 oz/200 g canned
   chopped tomatoes
1¼ cups fish stock
4 small striped bass or
   trout fillets
½ cup pitted green olives

1 tbsp chopped
   preserved lemon
3 tbsp chopped fresh
   cilantro
salt and pepper
freshly cooked couscous,
   to serve

Moroccan Fish Tagine

Heat the olive oil in a flameproof casserole. Add the onion and cook gently over very low heat, stirring occasionally, for 10 minutes, or until softened but not colored. Add the saffron, cinnamon, ground coriander, cumin, and turmeric and cook for an additional 30 seconds, stirring constantly.

Add the tomatoes and fish stock and stir well. Bring to a boil, reduce the heat, cover, and simmer for 15 minutes. Uncover and simmer for 20–35 minutes, or until thickened.

Cut each fish fillet in half, then add the fish pieces to the casserole, pushing them down into the liquid. Simmer the stew for an additional 5–6 minutes, or until the fish is just cooked.

Carefully stir in the olives, lemon, and fresh cilantro. Season to taste with salt and pepper and serve immediately with couscous.

SERVES 4

4 oz/115 g shrimp, peeled
9 oz/250 g prepared scallops, thawed if frozen
4 oz/115 g monkfish fillet, cut into chunks
1 lime, peeled and thinly sliced
1 tbsp chili powder
1 tsp ground cumin

3 tbsp chopped fresh cilantro
2 garlic cloves, finely chopped
1 fresh green chile, seeded and chopped
3 tbsp corn oil
1 onion, coarsely chopped
1 red and 1 yellow pepper, seeded and coarsely chopped

¼ tsp ground cloves
pinch of ground cinnamon
pinch of cayenne pepper
salt
1½ cups fish stock
14 oz/400 g canned chopped tomatoes
14 oz/400 g canned red kidney beans, drained and rinsed

Seafood Chili

Place the shrimp, scallops, monkfish chunks, and lime slices in a large, nonmetallic dish with ¼ teaspoon of the chili powder, ¼ teaspoon of the ground cumin, 1 tablespoon of the chopped cilantro, half the garlic, the fresh chile, and 1 tablespoon of the oil. Cover with plastic wrap and let marinate for up to 1 hour.

Meanwhile, heat 1 tablespoon of the remaining oil in a flameproof casserole or large, heavy-bottom pan. Add the onion, the remaining garlic, and the bell peppers and cook over low heat, stirring occasionally, for 5 minutes, or until softened.

Add the remaining chili powder, the remaining cumin, the cloves, cinnamon, and cayenne, with the remaining oil, if necessary, and season to taste with salt. Cook, stirring, for 5 minutes, then gradually stir in the stock and the tomatoes and their juice. Partially cover and simmer for 25 minutes.

Add the beans to the tomato mixture and spoon the fish and shellfish on top. Cover and cook for 10 minutes, or until the fish and shellfish are cooked through. Sprinkle with the remaining cilantro and serve.

SERVES 6

2 tbsp sunflower or corn oil
6 oz/175 g okra, trimmed and cut into 1-inch/2.5-cm pieces
2 onions, finely chopped
4 celery stalks, very finely chopped
1 garlic clove, finely chopped

2 tbsp all-purpose flour
½ tsp sugar
1 tsp ground cumin
3 cups fish stock
1 red bell pepper and 1 green bell pepper, seeded and chopped
2 large tomatoes, chopped

12 oz/350 g large shrimp
4 tbsp chopped fresh parsley
1 tbsp chopped fresh cilantro
dash of Tabasco sauce
12 oz/350 g striped bass or halibut fillets, skinned
salt and pepper

Louisiana Gumbo

Heat half the oil in a large, flameproof casserole or large pan with a tightly fitting lid, and cook the okra over low heat, stirring frequently, for 5 minutes, or until browned. Using a slotted spoon, remove the okra from the casserole and set aside.

Heat the remaining oil in the casserole and cook the onion and celery over medium heat, stirring frequently, for 5 minutes, or until softened. Add the garlic and cook, stirring, for 1 minute. Sprinkle in the flour, sugar, and cumin and season to taste with salt and pepper. Cook, stirring constantly, for 2 minutes, then remove from the heat.

Gradually stir in the stock and bring to a boil, stirring. Return the okra to the casserole and add the bell peppers and tomatoes. Partially cover, then reduce the heat to very low and simmer gently, stirring occasionally, for 10 minutes. Meanwhile, shell and devein the shrimp and reserve.

Add the herbs and Tabasco sauce to taste. Cut the cod and monkfish into 1-inch/2.5-cm chunks, then gently stir into the stew. Stir in the shrimp. Cover and simmer gently for 5 minutes, or until the fish is cooked through and the shrimp have turned pink. Transfer to a large, warmed serving dish and serve.

SERVES 4

2 tbsp vegetable oil
2 onions, coarsely chopped
1 green bell pepper, seeded and coarsely chopped
2 celery stalks, coarsely chopped
3 garlic cloves, finely chopped
2 tsp paprika

10½ oz/300 g skinless, boneless chicken breasts, chopped
3½ oz/100 g andouille or other smoked sausage, chopped
3 tomatoes, peeled and chopped
2 cups long-grain rice
3¾ cups hot chicken stock or fish stock

1 tsp dried oregano
2 bay leaves
12 large jumbo shrimp
4 scallions, finely chopped
2 tbsp chopped fresh parsley
salt and pepper
chopped fresh herbs, to garnish

Jambalaya

Heat the vegetable oil in a large skillet over low heat. Add the onions, bell pepper, celery, and garlic and cook for 8–10 minutes, until all the vegetables have softened. Add the paprika and cook for another 30 seconds. Add the chicken and sausages and cook for 8–10 minutes, until lightly browned. Add the tomatoes and cook for 2–3 minutes, until they have collapsed.

Add the rice to the pan and stir well. Add the hot stock, oregano, and bay leaves and stir well. Cover and simmer for 10 minutes.

Add the shrimp and stir well. Cover again and cook for another 6–8 minutes, until the rice is tender and the shrimp are cooked through.

Stir in the scallions and parsley and season to taste with salt and pepper. Remove the bay leaves, divide the jambalaya among 4 bowls, and serve garnished with chopped fresh herbs.

SERVES 4

1 tbsp olive oil
4 tbsp butter
2 garlic cloves, chopped
1¾ cups risotto rice
generous 5½ cups boiling
   fish or chicken stock

9 oz/250 g mixed cooked
   seafood, such as
   shrimp, squid, mussels,
   and clams
2 tbsp chopped fresh
   oregano, plus extra to
   garnish

½ cup freshly grated
   romano or Parmesan
   cheese
salt and pepper

Seafood Risotto

Heat the oil with half of the butter in a deep pan over medium heat until the butter has melted. Add the garlic and cook, stirring, for 1 minute.

Reduce the heat, add the rice, and mix to coat in oil and butter. Cook, stirring constantly, for 2–3 minutes, or until the grains are translucent.

Gradually add the hot stock, a ladleful at a time. Stir constantly and add more liquid as the rice absorbs each addition. Increase the heat to medium so that the liquid bubbles. Cook for 20 minutes, or until all the liquid is absorbed and the rice is creamy.

About 5 minutes before the rice is ready, add the seafood and oregano to the pan and mix well.

Remove the pan from the heat and season to taste with salt and pepper. Add the remaining butter and mix well, then stir in the grated cheese until it melts. Spoon onto warmed plates and serve at once, garnished with extra oregano.

SERVES 4

1 lb/450 g firm white fish fillets (such as striped bass or halibut), skinned and cut into 1-inch/2.5-cm cubes
2 tsp ground cumin
2 tsp dried oregano
2 tbsp lime juice
2/3 cup dark rum

1 tbsp dark brown sugar
3 garlic cloves, chopped finely
1 large onion, chopped
1 each medium red bell pepper, green bell pepper, and yellow bell pepper, seeded and sliced into rings

5 cups fish stock
1¾ cups long-grain rice
salt and pepper
fresh oregano leaves, to garnish
lime wedges, to garnish

Fish & Rice with Dark Rum

Place the cubes of fish in a bowl and add the cumin, oregano, lime juice, rum, and sugar. Season to taste with salt and pepper. Mix thoroughly, cover with plastic wrap, and set aside to chill for 2 hours.

Meanwhile, place the garlic, onion, and bell peppers in a large pan. Pour in the stock and stir in the rice. Bring to a boil, lower the heat, cover, and simmer for 15 minutes.

Gently stir in the fish and the marinade juices. Bring back to a boil and simmer, uncovered, stirring occasionally but being careful not to break up the fish, for about 10 minutes, until the fish is cooked and the rice is tender.

Taste and adjust the seasoning, if necessary, and divide among 4 bowls. Garnish with fresh oregano and lime wedges and serve.

SERVES 4

1 cup dried Chinese mushrooms

2 tbsp vegetable oil or peanut oil

6 scallions, chopped

scant ½ cup dry unsweetened coconut

1 fresh green chile, seeded and chopped

generous 1 cup jasmine rice

⅔ cup fish stock

1¾ cups coconut milk

12 oz/350 g cooked shelled shrimp

6 sprigs fresh Thai basil

Shrimp with Coconut Rice

Place the mushrooms in a small bowl, cover with hot water, and set aside to soak for 30 minutes. Drain, then cut off and discard the stalks and slice the caps.

Heat 1 tablespoon of the oil in a wok and stir-fry the scallions, coconut, and chile for 2–3 minutes, until lightly browned. Add the mushrooms and stir-fry for 3–4 minutes.

Add the rice and stir-fry for 2–3 minutes, then add the stock and bring to a boil. Reduce the heat and add the coconut milk. Let simmer for 10–15 minutes, until the rice is tender. Stir in the shrimp and basil, heat through, and serve.

SERVES 4-6

1 lb 8 oz/675 g prepared squid
3 tbsp olive oil
1 onion, finely chopped
3 garlic cloves, finely chopped

½ tsp thyme leaves
7 tbsp chopped flat-leaf parsley
½ cup white wine
1¼ cups canned chopped tomatoes

4 potatoes, cut into bite-size chunks
grated zest of 1 lemon
salt and pepper

Braised Squid with Potatoes, Lemon & Parsley

Slice the body of the squid crosswise into thin rings. Cut the rings in half if large. Slice the tentacles and wings into bite-size pieces.

Heat a Dutch oven over medium heat, add the oil, and gently cook the onion for about 10 minutes, until golden. Stir in the garlic, thyme, and 3 tablespoons of the parsley.

Add the squid and cook for 2-3 minutes, stirring, until opaque. Pour in the wine and simmer for 2 minutes, then add the tomatoes and ¼ teaspoon of pepper. Bring to a boil, then cover and simmer gently for 1-1½ hours until the squid is tender. Stir occasionally to prevent sticking, adding a little water, if necessary.

Add the potatoes to the pot and season to taste with salt and more pepper, if necessary. Cover and simmer for 20-30 minutes, or until the potatoes are tender but not breaking up.

Combine the lemon zest with the remaining parsley and add just before serving.

SERVES 4

½ cup golden raisins
5 tbsp olive oil
2 tbsp chopped fresh
  flat-leaf parsley, plus
  extra to garnish

2 garlic cloves, finely
  chopped
1 lb 12 oz/800 g
  prepared squid, sliced,
  or squid rings
½ cup dry white wine

2¼ cups tomato sauce
pinch of chili powder
¾ cup finely chopped
  pine nuts
salt

Squid with Parsley & Pine Nuts

Place the golden raisins in a small bowl, cover with lukewarm water, and set aside for 15 minutes to plump up.

Meanwhile, heat the olive oil in a heavy-bottom pan. Add the parsley and garlic and cook over low heat, stirring frequently, for 3 minutes. Add the squid and cook, stirring occasionally, for 5 minutes.

Increase the heat to medium, pour in the wine, and cook until it has almost completely evaporated. Stir in the tomato sauce and season to taste with chili powder and salt. Reduce the heat again, cover, and let simmer gently, stirring occasionally, for 45–50 minutes, until the squid is almost tender.

Drain the golden raisins and stir them into the pan with the pine nuts. Let simmer for an additional 10 minutes, then serve immediately garnished with the reserved chopped parsley.

SERVES 4

4 lb 8 oz/2 kg mussels
1¼ cups dry white wine

6 shallots, finely chopped
1 bouquet garni
pepper

4 bay leaves, to garnish
crusty bread, to serve

Moules Marinière

Clean the mussels by scrubbing or scraping the shells and pulling off any beards. Discard any with broken shells or any that refuse to close when tapped with a knife. Rinse the mussels under cold, running water.

Pour the wine into a large, heavy-bottom pan, add the shallots and bouquet garni, and season to taste with pepper. Bring to a boil over medium heat. Add the mussels, cover tightly, and cook, shaking the pan occasionally, for 5 minutes. Remove and discard the bouquet garni and any mussels that remain closed. Divide the mussels among 4 soup plates with a slotted spoon. Tilt the casserole to let any sediment settle, then spoon the cooking liquid over the mussels. Garnish with the bay leaves and serve immediately with bread.

Vegetarian

SERVES 6

2 tbsp olive oil
8 pearl onions, peeled
2 celery stalks, sliced
8 oz/225 g carrots, thickly
sliced
8 oz/225 g turnips, diced

generous ¼ cup pearl
barley, rinsed
3–3½ cups vegetable
stock
12 oz/350 g diced
Quorn®

¾ cup partially thawed
frozen peas
salt and pepper
1 tbsp chopped fresh
parsley, to garnish

Vegetable Pot

Preheat the oven to 350°F/180°C. Heat half the oil in a flameproof casserole dish over medium heat, add the onions, celery, carrots, and turnips, and cook for 10 minutes, stirring frequently. Add the pearl barley and cook for 1 minute, stirring occasionally, then pour in the stock and bring to a boil.

Season to taste with salt and pepper and cover. Cook in the preheated oven for 1–1¼ hours.

Meanwhile, heat the remaining oil in a skillet over medium heat, add the Quorn®, and cook, stirring frequently, for 5–8 minutes, or until golden.

Add the Quorn® to the casserole dish with the peas and cook in the oven for an additional 10–20 minutes, or until the vegetables are tender. Taste and adjust the seasoning and serve sprinkled with parsley.

SERVES 4

4 tbsp olive oil
1 tsp cumin seeds, crushed
1 onion, halved lengthwise and finely sliced into crescents
3 garlic cloves, finely chopped

½ fresh red chile, seeded and thinly sliced
1 lb/450 g green beans, trimmed and halved
2¾ cups canned chopped tomatoes and juice
1½ cups drained canned chickpeas, rinsed

finely grated zest of ½ lemon
3 tbsp chopped flat-leaf parsley
salt and pepper
warm pita, to serve

Spicy Green Beans, Chickpeas + Tomatoes

Heat a Dutch oven over medium heat. Add the oil and cumin seeds and sizzle for a few seconds to flavor the oil. Add the onion, reduce the heat to medium–low, and simmer for 10 minutes, until starting to color. Stir in the garlic and chile and cook for another minute.

Add the beans, increase the heat to medium, and stir for 3 minutes, until the beans are glossy and bright green. Season to taste with salt and pepper.

Stir in the tomatoes and chickpeas. Bring to a boil, then reduce the heat and simmer, covered, for 30–40 minutes, or until the beans are tender but not mushy. Taste and adjust the seasoning, if necessary, and stir in the lemon zest and parsley.

Serve hot, warm, or at room temperature, with plenty of warm pita to mop up the juices.

SERVES 4

2 eggplants
4 zucchini
2 yellow bell peppers
2 red bell peppers

2 onions
2 garlic cloves
2/3 cup olive oil
1 bouquet garni

3 large tomatoes, peeled,
   seeded, and coarsely
   chopped
salt and pepper

Classic Ratatouille

Coarsely chop the eggplant and zucchini, and seed and chop the bell peppers. Slice the onions and finely chop the garlic. Heat the oil in a large skillet. Add the onions and cook over low heat, stirring occasionally, for 5 minutes, or until softened. Add the garlic and cook, stirring frequently for an additional 2 minutes.

Add the eggplant, zucchini, and bell peppers. Increase the heat to medium and cook, stirring occasionally, until the bell peppers begin to color. Add the bouquet garni, reduce the heat, cover, and simmer gently for 40 minutes.

Stir in the chopped tomatoes and season to taste with salt and pepper. Re-cover the skillet and simmer gently for an additional 10 minutes. Remove and discard the bouquet garni. Serve warm or cold.

SERVES 4

2 tbsp olive oil
1 large Bermuda onion, sliced
2 bell peppers, any color, seeded and thinly sliced

2 zucchini, sliced into thin rounds
1 small eggplant, halved lengthwise and thinly sliced
2 garlic cloves, chopped

14 oz/400 g canned, crushed tomatoes with herbs, plus extra if needed
2 tsp smoked paprika
8 small eggs
salt and pepper

Ratatouille with Poached Eggs

Heat the oil in a large, lidded, nonstick skillet or shallow, flameproof casserole over medium–high heat, then add the onion and bell peppers and cook, stirring frequently, for 4–5 minutes, or until beginning to soften.

Add the zucchini, eggplant, and garlic and cook, stirring, for 2 minutes. Add the tomatoes, most of the paprika, and season to taste with salt and pepper. Stir and bring to a simmer. Reduce the heat to low, then cover and let simmer gently for 45 minutes, adding a little extra tomato or water if the mixture begins to look dry.

Make 8 wells in the ratatouille and break an egg into each. Re-cover and cook for an additional 10 minutes, or until the egg whites are cooked but the yolks still runny.

Serve immediately, garnished with paprika.

SERVES 4

1 tbsp olive oil
1 red onion, halved and sliced
3 garlic cloves, crushed
5 cups fresh spinach leaves
1 fennel bulb, cut into eighths

1 red bell pepper, seeded and diced
1 tbsp all-purpose flour
2 cups vegetable stock
⅓ cup dry white wine
14 oz/400 g canned chickpeas, drained
1 bay leaf

1 tsp ground coriander
½ tsp paprika
salt and pepper
fennel fronds, to garnish

Chickpea & Vegetable Stew

Heat the oil in a large, ovenproof casserole. Add the onion and garlic and sauté for 1 minute, stirring. Add the spinach and cook for 4 minutes, or until wilted.

Add the fennel and bell pepper and cook for 2 minutes, stirring. Stir in the flour and cook for 1 minute. Add the stock, wine, chickpeas, bay leaf, coriander, and paprika, then cover and cook for 30 minutes. Season to taste with salt and pepper, then garnish with fennel fronds and serve at once.

SERVES 4–8

1 lb 2 oz/500 g large flat
  mushrooms
2 tbsp oil
1 onion, sliced
1 red bell pepper, seeded
  and sliced

1 green bell pepper,
  seeded and sliced
1 garlic clove, crushed
¼–½ tsp cayenne pepper
juice and grated rind of
  2 limes

2 tsp sugar
1 tsp dried oregano
salt and pepper
8 flour tortillas
salsa, to serve

Mushroom Fajitas

Cut the mushrooms into strips. Heat the oil in a large, heavy-bottom skillet. Add the mushrooms, onions, bell peppers, and garlic, and stir-fry for 8–10 minutes, until the vegetables are cooked.

Add the cayenne pepper, lime juice and rind, sugar, and oregano. Season to taste with salt and pepper and cook for an additional 2 minutes.

Meanwhile, heat the tortillas according to the package instructions. Divide the mushroom mixture among the warmed tortillas and serve with the salsa.

SERVES 4

scant ½ cup olive oil
2 red onions, cut into
  8 wedges
3 garlic cloves, crushed
2 tsp ground cumin

2 tsp ground coriander
pinch of cayenne pepper
1 carrot, thickly sliced
2 small turnips, quartered
1 zucchini, sliced
4 potatoes, thickly sliced

juice and grated rind of
  2 large lemons
1¼ cups vegetable stock
2 tbsp chopped fresh
  cilantro
salt and pepper

Potato & Lemon Stew

Heat the olive oil in a flameproof casserole. Add the onions and sauté over medium heat, stirring frequently, for 3 minutes. Add the garlic and cook for 30 seconds. Stir in the ground cumin, ground coriander, and cayenne and cook, stirring constantly, for 1 minute. Add the carrot, turnips, zucchini, and potatoes and stir to coat in the oil.

Add the lemon juice and rind and the vegetable stock. Season to taste with salt and pepper. Cover and cook over medium heat, stirring occasionally, for 20–30 minutes, until tender.

Remove the lid, sprinkle in the chopped fresh cilantro, and stir well. Serve immediately.

SERVES 4

1 tbsp olive oil, for brushing
6 potatoes
2 leeks

2 beefsteak tomatoes
8 fresh basil leaves
1 garlic clove, finely chopped

1¼ cups vegetable stock
salt and pepper

Layered Vegetable Stew

Preheat the oven to 350°F/180°C. Brush a large flameproof dish with a little of the olive oil. Prepare all the vegetables. Peel and thinly slice the potatoes, trim and thinly slice the leeks, and slice the tomatoes.

Place a layer of potato slices in the bottom of the dish, sprinkle with half of the basil leaves, and cover with a layer of leeks. Top with a layer of tomato slices. Repeat these layers until all the vegetables are used up, ending with a layer of potatoes. Stir the chopped garlic into the vegetable stock and season to taste with salt and pepper. Pour the stock over the vegetables and brush the top with the remaining olive oil.

Bake in the preheated oven for 1½ hours, or until the vegetables are tender and the topping is golden brown. Serve immediately.

SERVES 4–6

1 onion, sliced
2 leeks, sliced
2 celery stalks, chopped
2 carrots, thinly sliced
1 red bell pepper, seeded
   and sliced
1¾ cups diced pumpkin

1⅔ cups diced mixed
   root vegetables, such
   as sweet potato,
   parsnip, and rutabaga
14 oz/400 g canned
   chopped tomatoes
⅔–1 cup hard cider

2 tsp dried Herbes de
   Provence
salt and pepper
chopped fresh herbs,
   to garnish
crusty bread, to serve

Root Vegetable + Pumpkin Stew

Preheat the oven to 350°F/180°C. Put the onion, leeks, celery, carrots, bell pepper, pumpkin, and root vegetables in a large casserole and mix well. Stir in the tomatoes, ⅔ cup of the hard cider, the dried herbs, mix well, and season to taste with salt and pepper.

Cover and bake in the center of the oven for 1¼–1½ hours, until the vegetables are cooked through and tender, stirring once or twice and adding a little extra hard cider, if necessary. Garnish with a sprinkling of chopped fresh herbs and serve with warm crusty bread.

SERVES 4

1 cup red lentils
generous ¼ cup long-
  grain rice
5 cups vegetable stock
1 leek, cut into chunks
3 garlic cloves, crushed
14 oz/400 g canned
  chopped tomatoes
1 tsp ground cumin

1 tsp chili powder
1 tsp garam masala
1 red bell pepper, seeded
  and sliced
1½ cups small broccoli
  florets
8 baby corn, halved
  lengthwise

½ cup halved green
  beans
1 tbsp shredded fresh
  basil
salt and pepper
fresh basil sprigs,
  to garnish

Lentil & Rice Stew

Place the lentils, rice, and vegetable stock in a large, flameproof casserole and cook over low heat, stirring occasionally, for 20 minutes.

Add the leek, garlic, tomatoes and their can juice, ground cumin, chili powder, garam masala, sliced bell pepper, broccoli, baby corn, and green beans to the casserole.

Bring the mixture to a boil, reduce the heat, cover, and simmer for an additional 10–15 minutes, or until all the vegetables are tender. Add the shredded basil and season to taste with salt and pepper. Serve immediately, garnished with the fresh basil sprigs.

SERVES 4

4 potatoes
1 leek, sliced
3 garlic cloves, crushed
scant ½ cup shredded
    cheddar cheese

scant ½ cup shredded
    mozzarella cheese
¼ cup freshly grated
    Parmesan cheese
2 tbsp chopped fresh
    flat-leaf parsley

⅔ cup light cream
⅔ cup milk
salt and pepper

Cheese + Potato Layered Casserole

Preheat the oven to 325°F/160°C. Cook the potatoes in a pan of lightly salted boiling water for 10 minutes. Drain well.

Cut the potatoes into thin slices. Arrange a layer of potatoes in the bottom of an ovenproof dish. Layer with a little of the leek, garlic, cheeses, and chopped parsley and season to taste with salt and pepper.

Repeat the layers until all of the ingredients have been used, finishing with a layer of cheese on top.

Mix the cream and milk together and season to taste with salt and pepper, then pour the mixture over the potato layers. Cook in the oven for 1–1¼ hours, or until the cheese is golden brown and bubbling and the potatoes are cooked through. Serve immediately.

SERVES 4

1 small head of cauliflower, broken into florets
2 large potatoes, cubed
6 cherry tomatoes

sauce
2 tbsp butter or margarine
1 leek, sliced
1 garlic clove, crushed
2 tbsp all-purpose flour
1¼ cups milk

scant ¾ cup mixed shredded or grated cheese, such as cheddar, Parmesan, and Gruyère cheese
½ tsp paprika
2 tbsp chopped fresh flatleaf parsley, plus extra to garnish
salt and pepper

Cauliflower Bake

Preheat the oven to 350°F/180°C. Cook the cauliflower in a pan of boiling water for 10 minutes. Drain well and set aside. Meanwhile, cook the potatoes in a separate pan of boiling water for 10 minutes, drain, and set aside.

To make the sauce, melt the butter or margarine in a pan. Add the leek and garlic and sauté for 1 minute. Add the flour and cook for 1 minute. Remove the pan from the heat and gradually stir in the milk, scant ½ cup of the cheese, the paprika, and parsley. Return the pan to the heat. Bring to a boil, stirring. Season to taste with salt and pepper.

Spoon the cauliflower into a deep, ovenproof dish. Add the tomatoes and top with the potatoes. Pour the sauce over the potatoes and sprinkle with the remaining grated cheese.

Cook in the oven for 20 minutes, or until the vegetables are cooked through and the cheese is golden brown and bubbling. Garnish with parsley and serve at once.

SERVES 2

4 tbsp olive oil
2 onions, finely chopped
2 garlic cloves, very finely
    chopped

2 eggplants, thickly sliced
3 tbsp fresh flat-leaf
    parsley, chopped

½ tsp dried thyme
14 oz/400 g canned
    chopped tomatoes

Eggplant Gratin

Preheat the oven to 400°F/200°C. Heat the oil in a flameproof casserole over medium heat. Add the onions and cook for 5 minutes, or until soft. Add the garlic and cook for a few seconds, or until just beginning to color. Using a slotted spoon, transfer the onion mixture to a plate.

Cook the eggplant slices in batches in the same flameproof casserole until they are just lightly browned. Transfer to another plate.

Arrange a layer of eggplant slices in the bottom of the casserole dish. Sprinkle with the parsley, thyme, and salt and pepper.

Add a layer of onion, tomatoes, and mozzarella, sprinkling parsley, thyme, and salt and pepper over each layer.

Continue layering, finishing with a layer of eggplant slices. Sprinkle with the Parmesan. Bake, uncovered, for 20–30 minutes, or until the top is golden and the eggplant slices are tender. Serve hot.

SERVES 4-6

4 tbsp butter
6 zucchini, sliced
2 cups shredded Gruyère
  cheese or grated
  Parmesan cheese

2 tbsp chopped fresh
  tarragon or a mixture
  of mint, tarragon, and
  flat-leaf parsley
½ cup milk

½ cup heavy cream
2 eggs
freshly grated nutmeg
salt and pepper

Zucchini & Cheese Gratin

Preheat the oven to 350°F/180°C. Melt the butter in a large sauté pan or skillet over medium-high heat. Add the zucchini and sauté for 4-6 minutes, turning the slices over occasionally, until colored on both sides. Remove from the pan and drain on paper towels, then season to taste with salt and pepper.

Spread half the zucchini over the bottom of a greased ovenproof serving dish. Sprinkle with ½ cup of the cheese and half the herbs. Repeat these layers once more.

Mix the milk, cream, and eggs together and season with nutmeg, salt, and pepper. Pour this liquid over the zucchini, then sprinkle the top with the remaining cheese.

Bake the gratin in the preheated oven for 40 minutes, or until it is set in the center and golden brown. Remove from the oven and let stand for 5 minutes before serving straight from the dish.

SERVES 4

1 cauliflower, cut into florets
4 tbsp butter
1²/₃ cups sliced mushrooms
salt and pepper

topping
1²/₃ cups dry breadcrumbs
2 tbsp grated Parmesan cheese

1 tsp dried oregano
1 tsp dried parsley
2 tbsp butter

Mushroom & Cauliflower Cheese Crumble

Preheat the oven to 450°F/230°C. Bring a large saucepan of lightly salted water to a boil. Add the cauliflower and cook for 3 minutes. Remove from the heat, drain well, and transfer to a shallow, ovenproof dish.

Melt the butter in a small skillet over medium heat. Add the mushrooms, stir, and cook gently for 3 minutes. Remove from the heat and spoon on top of the cauliflower. Season to taste with salt and pepper. Combine the breadcrumbs, Parmesan, and herbs in a small bowl, then sprinkle over the vegetables.

Dice the butter and dot over the breadcrumb mixture. Bake in the preheated oven for 15 minutes, or until the topping is golden brown.

SERVES 4–6

3 parsnips
4 large carrots
butter for greasing
1¾ cups chicken or
   vegetable stock

1¾ cups heavy cream
2 large garlic cloves,
   flattened with a heavy
   knife blade

freshly grated nutmeg
salt and pepper

Peppery Parsnip & Carrot Gratin

Preheat the oven to 350°F/180°C. Slice the parsnips and carrots, and place in a steamer basket set over boiling water. Steam for 3–4 minutes, until tender. Butter a large gratin dish, and arrange the vegetables in it.

Heat the stock and cream in a saucepan with the garlic. Season to taste with salt and pepper and two good pinches of nutmeg.

Pour the hot cream mixture over the vegetables. Cover the dish with foil and bake for 30 minutes. Remove the foil and bake for another 20–25 minutes, or until golden on top. Sprinkle with a little more nutmeg and pepper before serving.

SERVES 4

1 large fennel bulb
2 tbsp olive oil
1 red onion, cut into small wedges
2–4 garlic cloves, sliced
1 fresh green chile, seeded and chopped
1 small eggplant, cut into chunks
2 tbsp tomato paste

scant 2–2½ cups vegetable stock
4 tomatoes
1 tbsp balsamic vinegar
a few sprigs of fresh oregano
14 oz/400 g canned borlotti beans
14 oz/400 g canned flageolets

1 yellow bell pepper, seeded and cut into small strips
1 zucchini, sliced into half moons
⅓ cup pitted black olives
1 oz/25 g Parmesan cheese, freshly shaved
salt and pepper
crusty bread, to serve

Tuscan Bean Stew

Trim the fennel and reserve any feathery fronds, then cut the bulb into small strips. Heat the oil in a large, heavy-bottom pan with a tight-fitting lid, and cook the onion, garlic, chile, and fennel strips, stirring frequently, for 5–8 minutes, or until softened.

Add the eggplant and cook, stirring frequently, for 5 minutes. Blend the tomato paste with a little of the stock in a pitcher and pour over the fennel mixture, then add the remaining stock and the tomatoes, vinegar, and oregano. Bring to a boil, then reduce the heat and simmer, covered, for 15 minutes, or until the tomatoes have begun to collapse.

Drain and rinse the beans, then drain again. Add them to the pan with the yellow bell pepper, zucchini, and olives. Simmer for an additional 15 minutes, or until the vegetables are tender. Taste and adjust the seasoning, if necessary. Scatter with the Parmesan shavings and serve garnished with the reserved fennel fronds, accompanied by crusty bread.

SERVES 6

1 tbsp olive oil
1 onion, finely chopped
1 garlic clove, finely
    chopped
1 carrot, halved and
    thinly sliced

1 small head of green
    cabbage, cored,
    quartered, and thinly
    sliced
14 oz/400 g canned
    chopped tomatoes
½ tsp dried thyme
2 bay leaves

6¼ cups chicken stock or
    vegetable stock
1 cup green lentils
2 cups water
salt and pepper
chopped fresh parsley,
    to garnish

Vegetable Stew with Green Lentils

Heat the oil in a large saucepan over medium heat, add the onion, garlic, and carrot and cook for 3–4 minutes, stirring frequently, until the onion starts to soften. Add the cabbage and cook for an additional 2 minutes.

Add the tomatoes, thyme, and 1 bay leaf, then pour in the stock. Bring to a boil, reduce the heat to low, and cook gently, partially covered, for about 45 minutes, until the vegetables are tender.

Meanwhile, put the lentils in another saucepan with the remaining bay leaf and the water. Bring just to a boil, reduce the heat, and simmer for about 25 minutes, until tender. Drain off any remaining water, and set aside.

Let the vegetables cool slightly, then transfer to a food processor or blender and process until smooth, working in batches, if necessary. (If using a food processor, strain off the cooking liquid and reserve. Puree the soup solids with enough cooking liquid to moisten them, then combine with the remaining liquid.)

Return the stew to the saucepan and add the cooked lentils. Taste and adjust the seasoning, if necessary, and cook for about 10 minutes to heat through. Ladle into warmed bowls and garnish with parsley.

SERVES 4

4 garlic cloves
1 small acorn squash
1 red onion, sliced
2 leeks, sliced
1 eggplant, sliced
1 small celeriac, diced
2 turnips, sliced
2 plum tomatoes,
    chopped
1 carrot, sliced

1 zucchini, sliced
2 red bell peppers
1 fennel bulb, sliced
6 oz/175 g Swiss chard
2 bay leaves
½ tsp fennel seeds
½ tsp chili powder
pinch each of dried
    thyme, dried oregano,
    and sugar

½ cup extra virgin olive oil
scant 1 cup vegetable
    stock
⅔ cup torn fresh basil
    leaves
4 tbsp chopped fresh
    parsley
salt and pepper
2 tbsp freshly grated
    Parmesan cheese,
    to serve

Italian Vegetable Stew

Finely chop the garlic and dice the squash. Put them in a large, heavy-bottom pan with a tight-fitting lid. Add the onion, leeks, eggplant, celeriac, turnips, tomatoes, carrot, zucchini, bell peppers, fennel, Swiss chard, bay leaves, fennel seeds, chili powder, thyme, oregano, sugar, oil, stock, and half the basil to the pan. Mix together well, then bring to a boil.

Reduce the heat, then cover and simmer for 30 minutes, or until all the vegetables are tender.

Sprinkle in the remaining basil and the parsley and season to taste with salt and pepper. Serve immediately, sprinkled with the cheese.

SERVES 4

1 tbsp olive oil
1 garlic clove, crushed
8 small onions, halved
2 celery stalks, sliced
1¾ cups chopped
   rutabaga
2 carrots, sliced
½ small head of
   cauliflower, broken into
   florets
3¼ cups sliced button
   mushrooms

14 oz/400 g canned
   chopped tomatoes
¼ cup red lentils, rinsed
2 tbsp cornstarch
3–4 tbsp water
1¼ cups vegetable stock
2 tsp Tabasco sauce
2 tsp chopped fresh
   oregano
fresh oregano sprigs,
   for garnish

topping
heaping 1½ cups
   self-rising flour
pinch of salt
4 tbsp butter
scant 1¼ cups shredded
   sharp cheddar cheese
2 tsp chopped fresh
   oregano
1 egg, lightly beaten
⅔ cup milk

Winter Vegetable Cobbler

Preheat the oven to 350°F/180°C. Heat the oil in a large skillet and cook the garlic and onions over low heat for 5 minutes. Add the celery, rutabaga, carrots, and cauliflower and cook for 2–3 minutes.

Add the mushrooms, tomatoes, and lentils. Place the cornstarch and water in a bowl and mix to make a smooth paste. Stir into the skillet with the stock, Tabasco, and oregano. Transfer to an ovenproof dish, cover, and bake in the preheated oven for 20 minutes.

To make the topping, sift the flour and salt into a bowl. Rub in the butter, then stir in most of the cheese and the chopped oregano. Beat the egg with the milk in a small bowl and add enough to the dry ingredients to make a soft dough. Knead, then roll out to ½ inch/1 cm thick and cut into 2-inch/5-cm circles.

Remove the dish from the oven and increase the temperature to 400°F/200°C. Arrange the dough circles around the edge of the dish, brush with the remaining egg-and-milk mixture, and sprinkle with the reserved cheese. Cook for an additional 10–12 minutes. Garnish with oregano sprigs and serve.

SERVES 4

¼ cup sun-dried tomatoes, chopped
1 cup French green lentils
2½ cups cold water
2 tbsp olive oil
½–1 tsp dried chile flakes
2–3 garlic cloves, chopped
1 large onion, cut into small wedges

1 small celeriac, cut into small chunks
4 carrots, sliced
5 small new potatoes, scrubbed and cut into chunks
1 small acorn squash, seeded, peeled, and cut into small chunks

2 tbsp tomato paste
1¼ cups vegetable stock
1–2 tsp hot paprika
few fresh sprigs of thyme
1 lb/450 g ripe tomatoes
sour cream and crusty bread, to serve

Vegetable Goulash

Put the sun-dried tomatoes in a small heatproof bowl, then cover with almost boiling water and let soak for 15–20 minutes. Drain, reserving the soaking liquid. Meanwhile, rinse and drain the lentils, then put them in a pan with the cold water and bring to a boil. Reduce the heat, then cover and simmer for 15 minutes. Drain and set aside.

Heat the oil in a large, heavy-bottom pan with a tight-fitting lid and cook the chile flakes, garlic, and vegetables, stirring frequently, for 5–8 minutes, or until softened. Blend the tomato paste with a little of the stock in a pitcher and pour over the vegetable mixture, then add the remaining stock, lentils, the sun-dried tomatoes and their soaking liquid, and the paprika and thyme.

Bring to a boil, then reduce the heat and simmer, covered, for 15 minutes. Add the fresh tomatoes and simmer for an additional 15 minutes, or until the vegetables and lentils are tender. Serve topped with spoonfuls of sour cream, accompanied by crusty bread.

SERVES 4

1 eggplant, cut into 1-inch/2.5-cm slices
1 tbsp olive oil, plus extra for brushing
1 large red or yellow onion, finely chopped
2 red or yellow bell peppers, seeded and finely chopped
3–4 garlic cloves, finely chopped or crushed

1 lb 12 oz/800 g canned chopped tomatoes
1 tbsp mild chili powder
½ tsp ground cumin
½ tsp dried oregano
2 small zucchini, cut into fourths lengthwise and sliced
14 oz/400 g canned kidney beans, drained and rinsed

scant 2 cups water
1 tbsp tomato paste
salt and pepper
6 scallions, finely chopped, to garnish
scant 1¼ cups shredded cheddar cheese, to serve
crusty bread, to serve

Vegetable Chili

Brush the eggplant slices on one side with oil. Heat half the oil in a large, heavy-bottom skillet. Add the eggplant slices, oiled-side up, and cook over medium heat for 5–6 minutes, or until browned on one side. Turn the slices over, cook on the other side until browned, and transfer to a plate. Cut into bite-size pieces.

Heat the remaining oil in a large pan over medium heat. Add the chopped onion and bell peppers to the pan and cook, stirring occasionally, for 3–4 minutes, or until the onion is just softened but not browned. Add the garlic and cook for an additional 2–3 minutes, or until the onion just begins to color.

Add the tomatoes, chili powder, cumin, and oregano. Season to taste with salt and pepper. Bring just to a boil, reduce the heat, cover, and simmer gently for 15 minutes.

Add the zucchini, eggplant, and kidney beans. Stir in the water and tomato paste. Return to a boil, then cover the pan and simmer for an additional 45 minutes, or until the vegetables are tender. Taste and adjust the seasoning, if necessary.

Ladle into warmed bowls, garnish with the scallions, and serve sprinkled with cheese and with the crusty bread on the side.

SERVES 4

1 eggplant
2 turnips
8 small new potatoes
½ small head of
  cauliflower
8 oz/225 g button
  mushrooms
1 large onion
3 carrots
6 tbsp ghee or vegetable
  oil

2 garlic cloves, crushed
4 tsp chopped ginger
1–2 fresh green chiles,
  seeded and chopped
1 tbsp paprika
2 tsp ground coriander
1 tbsp mild or medium
  curry powder
2 cups vegetable stock

14 oz/400 g canned
  chopped tomatoes
1 green bell pepper,
  seeded and sliced
1 tbsp cornstarch
⅔ cup coconut milk
salt
fresh cilantro sprigs,
  to garnish
freshly cooked rice,
  to serve

Mixed Vegetable Curry

Cut the eggplant, turnips, and potatoes into ½-inch/1-cm cubes. Break the cauliflower into small florets. Leave the mushrooms whole if small or slice them thickly, if preferred. Slice the onion and carrots.

Heat the ghee in a large saucepan over low heat. Add the onion, turnips, potatoes, and cauliflower and cook, stirring frequently, for 3 minutes.

Add the garlic, ginger, chiles, paprika, ground coriander, and curry powder and cook, stirring constantly, for 1 minute.

Add the stock, tomatoes, eggplant, and mushrooms, and season to taste with salt. Cover and simmer, stirring occasionally, for 30 minutes, or until tender. Add the bell pepper and carrots, cover, and cook for an additional 5 minutes.

Put the cornstarch and coconut milk in a bowl, mix into a smooth paste, and stir into the vegetable mixture. Simmer, stirring constantly, for 2 minutes. Taste and adjust the seasoning, if necessary. Transfer to serving bowls, garnish with cilantro sprigs, and serve at once with freshly cooked rice.

SERVES 6

2 tbsp olive oil or vegetable oil
generous 1 cup risotto rice
2 garlic cloves, crushed
1 onion, chopped
2 celery stalks, chopped
1 red or green bell pepper, seeded and chopped

3¼ cups thinly sliced button mushrooms
1 tbsp chopped fresh oregano or 1 tsp dried oregano
4 cups boiling vegetable stock
¼ cup sun-dried tomatoes in olive oil, drained and chopped (optional)

½ cup finely grated Parmesan cheese
salt and pepper
fresh flat-leaf parsley sprigs, to garnish

Parmesan Risotto with Mushrooms

Heat the oil in a large, deep skillet. Add the rice and cook over low heat, stirring constantly, for 2–3 minutes, until the grains are thoroughly coated in oil and translucent.

Add the garlic, onion, celery, and bell pepper and cook, stirring frequently, for 5 minutes. Add the mushrooms and cook for 3–4 minutes. Stir in the oregano.

Gradually add the hot stock, a ladleful at a time. Stir constantly and add more liquid as the rice absorbs each addition. Increase the heat to medium so that the liquid bubbles. Cook for 20 minutes, or until all the liquid is absorbed and the rice is creamy. Add the sun-dried tomatoes, if using, 5 minutes before the end of the cooking time, then season to taste with salt and pepper.

Remove the risotto from the heat and stir in half the Parmesan until it melts. Transfer the risotto to warmed bowls. Top with the remaining cheese, garnish with flat-leaf parsley, and serve at once.

SERVES 4–6

½ tsp saffron threads
2 tbsp hot water
6 tbsp olive oil
1 Bermuda onion, sliced
3 garlic cloves, minced
1 red bell pepper, seeded and sliced

1 orange bell pepper, seeded and sliced
1 large eggplant, cubed
1 cup medium-grain paella rice
2½ cups vegetable stock
4 tomatoes, peeled and chopped

½ cups sliced button mushrooms
1 cup halved green beans
14 oz/400 g canned pinto beans
salt and pepper

Vegetarian Paella

Put the saffron threads and water in a small bowl or cup and let steep for a few minutes.

Meanwhile, heat the oil in a paella pan or wide, shallow skillet and cook the onion over medium heat, stirring, for 2–3 minutes, or until softened. Add the garlic, bell peppers, and eggplant and cook, stirring frequently, for 5 minutes.

Add the rice and cook, stirring constantly, for 1 minute, or until glossy and coated. Pour in the stock, add the tomatoes and saffron and its soaking water, and season to taste with salt and pepper. Bring to a boil, then reduce the heat and let simmer, shaking the skillet frequently and stirring occasionally, for 15 minutes.

Stir in the mushrooms, green beans, and pinto beans with their can juices. Cook for an additional 10 minutes, then serve immediately.

SERVES 4–6

scant 1¼ cups basmati rice
2 tbsp ghee, vegetable oil, or peanut oil
5 green cardamom pods, bruised

5 cloves
½ cinnamon stick
1 tsp fennel seeds
½ tsp black mustard seeds
2 bay leaves

2 cups water
1½ tsp salt
2 tbsp chopped fresh cilantro
pepper

Spiced Basmati Rice

Rinse the basmati rice in several changes of water until the water runs clear, then let soak for 30 minutes. Drain and set aside until ready to cook.

Melt the ghee in a flameproof casserole or a large saucepan with a tight-fitting lid over medium–high heat. Add the spices and bay leaves and stir for 30 seconds. Stir the rice into the casserole so the grains are coated with ghee. Stir in the water and salt and bring to a boil.

Reduce the heat to as low as possible and cover the casserole tightly. Simmer, without lifting the lid, for 8–10 minutes, until the grains are tender and all the liquid is absorbed.

Turn off the heat and use two forks to mix in the cilantro. Taste and adjust the seasoning, if necessary. Re-cover the pan and let stand for 5 minutes.